# The Student Nurse's Guide to Successful Reflection

## Ten Essential Ingredients

Hope this helps you to be the best version of you :)
N. Clarke
Nov 23

# The Student Nurse's Guide to Successful Reflection

## Ten Essential Ingredients

*Nicola Clarke*

Open University Press

Open University Press
McGraw-Hill Education
8th Floor, 338 Euston Road
London
England
NW1 3BH

email: enquiries@openup.co.uk
world wide web: www.openup.co.uk

and Two Penn Plaza, New York, NY 10121-2289, USA

First published 2017

Copyright © Nicola Clarke, 2017

All rights reserved. Except for the quotation of short passages for the purposes of criticism and review, no part of this publication may be reproduced, stored in a retrieval system, or transmitted, in any form or by any means, electronic, mechanical, photocopying, recording or otherwise, without the prior written permission of the publisher or a licence from the Copyright Licensing Agency Limited. Details of such licences (for reprographic reproduction) may be obtained from the Copyright Licensing Agency Ltd of Saffron House, 6–10 Kirby Street, London EC1N 8TS.

A catalogue record of this book is available from the British Library

ISBN-13: 978-0-335-26228-1
ISBN-10: 0-33-526228-7
eISBN: 978-0-335-26229-8

Library of Congress Cataloging-in-Publication Data
CIP data applied for

Typeset by Transforma Pvt. Ltd., Chennai, India

Printed and bound by CPI Group (UK) Ltd, Croydon, CR0 4YY

Fictitious names of companies, products, people, characters and/or data that may be used herein (in case studies or in examples) are not intended to represent any real individual, company, product or event.

# Praise for this book

*"Reflection is a 'way of being' encompassing many ingredients. Clarke, with great thoroughness and care, introduces these, constructively supporting students towards developing self-insight and understanding of others. Her advice, explanations, illustrations and exercises are lucid and paced, helping nurses towards sufficient strength to undertake the developmental change which effective reflective practice brings. And to become practitioners who are far more than competent: nurses who are calmly self-aware, receptive and perceptive."*

*Gillie Bolton, PhD, former Senior Research Fellow, Medicine and the Arts, King's College London, UK*

*"Reflection is a much discussed topic in nursing, but some students find it difficult to reflect on their own practice. Nicola Clarke's ten essential ingredients provide a clear and explicit guide to effective reflective practice and as such this should be a key text for all student nurses. The chapters of this new text offer clear learning outcomes, practical advice and models to follow in order to develop a genuine, honest and balanced reflective writing style. It is an engaging and informative read which promotes understanding of this important process."*

*Anita Savage Grainge, RMN, RGN, RNT, Senior Lecturer, University of York, UK*

*"An engaging book, which deals with the complexity of reflection in a clear, logical and in-depth manner. Developed around her extended definition of reflective practice, Clarke clearly and logically enables the reader to build their understanding of reflective practice by focusing on her ten ingredients. The structure of the book, focusing on two ingredients in each chapter, allows Clarke to provide clarity whilst at the same time showing the reader how the ingredients fit together to build a whole*

*that is greater than the sum of its parts. The focus on critical and analytic skills as well as person-centredness based on Rogers' core conditions provides a strong theoretical basis for students to understand reflective practice. The use of questions and examples throughout are engaging and will be useful for students and tutors alike.*

*I think this book will be excellent for all healthcare workers – students and qualified alike. Whilst it is aimed at nurses, the principles apply across healthcare. I think it is a real gem and certainly the best book I have read about reflective practice."*

*Dr Rosie Stenhouse, Nursing Studies, University of Edinburgh, UK*

*"Readers, I anticipate, will find this book informative, challenging and rewarding. It will, however, require focus and concentration to absorb and digest the considerable information the author has gleaned over many years. The book draws on extensive reading, research, teaching and observation of how individuals grow and develop as a result of adopting reflection into their daily lives. Warming to the style and content of the book, I was relieved to find that, unlike some others that approach the same topic, it does not purport to convey the essence and benefits of reflection by utilising inaccessible language, relying on unintelligible descriptions and conflating disparate models to a point where students are left bewildered and at a loss to know how to start their reflective practice. Much of the appeal of this book is that it is clearly written, logically presented and readily accessible, avoiding the jargon that sometimes characterises narratives about reflection. The reader will be impressed by the thoughtful layout which is designed to show that the acquisition of knowledge is not reducible to a set of simple tasks. It is the result of being able to manage the process of deepening one's understanding of reflection, internalising its values and cognitive practices and applying its behavioural components to the various forms of engagement that nurses enter into in the course of their work. Acquiring self-knowledge is not a one-off activity, but a life-long incremental process.*

*Three voices permeate the text – that of students, theorists and the author – each providing different perspectives which are skilfully integrated. The text could be used by students working alone or in groups, or it could provide thematic material running across several modules. While informative, it is not prescriptive. Students are encouraged to undertake exercises which are designed to deepen their understanding of and internalise what they have learned whilst constantly analysing what reflection means to them and how they elect to put it into practice. I was especially pleased to see the importance of emotions in the learning process recognised and how Socratic learning methods can become part of the behavioural repertoire of the student. A subtext in the book relates to inclining students to assume responsibility for their own learning which requires them to realise what it is that has to be achieved and recognise when it has been attained.*

*I was impressed by this book and the conversational tone of the narrative. It recognises that the learning mind is vulnerable and that inducting students into exploring what it is to be human is one of the highest forms of care. I imagine that important reasons for writing this book at this time are the ever-expanding content of curricula, the excessive demands on lecturing staff, and the relentless pressure in clinical settings which mean that many staff do not have the time to stand back, take stock and review where they have got to. I believe Nicola Clarke has made a significant contribution to nursing literature in highlighting an aspect of learning that can only become more important as further changes take place in health care provision. This text would be high on my reading list were I to start my nurse training over again."*

*Peter Nolan, Professor of Mental Health Nursing (Emeritus)*

*"Reflection is often a misunderstood concept for nursing staff. This book demystifies what is essentially a complex subject and makes it accessible in an easy to read format.*

*Nicola Clarke's passion for reflection shines throughout this book. As you progress there are a number of exercises and action points which allow you to experience the reflection process in your own learning. This is supplemented with case studies which bring the learning to life. Each chapter also*

***benefits from a succinct end of chapter summary to reinforce your understanding.***

***I would like to commend the author as this is a well-timed addition to the body of knowledge for mental health nursing students and is relevant now as it will be in the future. I would recommend this book to all nurses and I will be referring my students to this book as an essential text on their journey to discover their reflective voice."***

*Manyara N Mushore, Course Director, BSc Mental Health Nursing, London South Bank University, UK*

# Contents

# Foreword

It is a genuine pleasure to write a few words to introduce the reader to *The Student Nurse's Guide to Successful Reflection.* I remember being a student nurse (many years ago) – and what I acutely remember more than anything else are the mistakes I made. These were mistakes both in my academic learning and in my practice. I came to gradually realize that we all make mistakes and that making a mistake is not the end of the world. But at the time, I felt embarrassment, shame, and guilt. What is most important, however, is what we do next, once the mistake has been made. This is where successful reflection is imperative. But, of course, reflective practice is not just about dwelling on our mistakes – it is also about celebrating our achievements. More than that, reflection involves stopping and thinking about and questioning the routines and practices we exercise every minute of every working day, whether we consider them achievements or failures.

In this book, Nicola Clarke does a thorough job in explaining the elements of reflective practice. While reflection requires thinking skills, it is not merely an academic exercise. In the process of reflection, we are doing the most important aspect of nursing practice. Arguably, it is through the process of reflection that we truly learn. This learning is not only good practice, but it is vital for individual development and retaining the standards of the nursing profession. Among other things, reflective practice requires self-awareness. Long experience informs me that people who declare that they are self-aware are the ones who are not. In this book, the reader is led on a journey to learn, grow, and develop self-awareness. No book can enable a person to become self-aware, but a book can make a person think, question, and learn. This book can provide the opportunity, but only the reader can do something about it.

So, I urge you to take this book seriously and take it to your heart as well as your head. Nursing is an extraordinary profession where each one of us is expected to be an extraordinary person. It is in the art of being human we may find the art of being a good nurse. At the heart of this art is the need for reflective practice. This book will help you to learn how to be reflective and, importantly, how to be a better nurse.

Theo Stickley
Associate Professor, University of Nottingham, UK

# Acknowledgements

First and foremost I would like to thank all of the students and members of staff who took part in my original research for my Educational Doctorate. These individuals provided me with the rich data I needed to generate the ideas that underpin the extended description of, and the new approach to reflection and reflective practice that this book is based upon.

I would like to thank my colleagues, students and friends whom I have worked with over the past fourteen years at Birmingham City University, for providing me with an environment of academic debate and discussion and for listening to me talk at length at times about reflection; For challenging my thinking about reflection when I needed to see other perspectives.

I would like to thank in particular those, friends, colleagues and students who have supported me in my endeavours to write this book by reading chapters for me and acting as my much needed critical friends.

I would also like to thank the editorial team at McGraw Hill Education for their support in their diligent editing of my chapters.

I would like to offer a special thank you to Mark Stevens, my mentor, and friend who introduced to me to this world of reflection.

I cannot thank people without giving a special mention to my mum and dad whom have always had faith in me, where I may have not and for supporting me through years and years of study both emotionally and monetary. For being superb role models both as people and as parents.

My partner, John Findlay also gets a mention, his support for me in writing this book has been unwavering and persistent at times when I wanted to give up.

Finally, I have an amazing daughter and although she has no idea what I do, or what reflection is, she has asked me every day "how are you getting on with your book mummy", and this is all I have needed.

# An introduction to the Author

The author of this book is Nicola Clarke, EdD and Senior Fellow of the Higher Education Academy. Nicola is a mental health nurse with a background in substance misuse nursing. As a senior lecturer with over 14 years' experience teaching mental health nursing, academic skills, reflection and reflective writing, her current role has expanded to that of doctoral supervisor and examiner.

Nicola has always had a passion for reflection and reflective practice stemming from her experiences as a student mental health nurse, being mentored by an exceptional nurse who helped instil a desire for self-development. As a result Nicola undertook her MSc in General Psychiatry and following on from this her Educational Doctorate where she focused her efforts on learning and learning contexts, giving rise to her research focus of, understanding the teaching and learning experiences of students and staff in relation to reflection and reflective practice. Having spent nine years immersing herself in the subject of reflection, Nicola wanted to write a book that would be more than a theoretical underpinning of reflection, a book that would be useful to the students, accessible and easy to read. A book that would ensure the student would be able to reflect on the conclusion of the final chapter. The results of her research from her doctorate produced a new extended description of and a new approach to reflection. It is this description and approach that is the foundation of this book.

Nicola has one daughter, two step children, a partner and a very lazy greyhound. She has a passion for dancing, pole fitness and in her spare time helps her partner run combat robot events around the country.

CHAPTER

# Introduction: beginning our journey into reflection

## Learning outcomes

By the end of this chapter, you will be able to:

- Understand the notion of reflection
- Understand how reflection becomes reflective practice
- Recognize the importance of reflection and reflective practice
- Know when to reflect.

## Introduction

How many times have you wished you could do things differently? How many times have you wished you could change the way you are, or change the way you think and feel? Consider the following passage featuring a familiar character:

> Here is Edward Bear, coming downstairs now, bump, bump, bump, on the back of his head, behind Christopher Robin. It is, as far as he knows, the only way of coming downstairs, but sometimes he feels that there really is another way, if only he could stop bumping for a moment and think of it.
>
> (Winnie the Pooh, in Milne 1973: 49)

How often have you said 'there must be another way?', just like Winnie the Pooh? Have you ever spent too much time worrying about something that has happened that may or may not have been your fault? Do you always learn from the things you do well and the things you do not so well?

Reflection and reflective practice is the key to learning about you, to gaining heightened levels of self-awareness, to enhancing your emotional intelligence. Reflection and reflective practice will help you to choose whether to repeat the same behaviour, to make informed decisions as to whether you need to adapt to different circumstances and experiences you have, and to find other potentially better ways of doing things.

I would therefore like to warmly welcome you to *The Student Nurse's Guide to Successful Reflection*. The aim of this book is to support you in developing the necessary skills and attitude for successful reflection, but more importantly engender a 'way of being' that naturalizes the reflective process for you and hopefully instils a sense of passion towards reflective practice – with the ultimate aim of fostering a level of emotional intelligence that allows us as practitioners to be able to use ourselves therapeutically, and employ our emotional intelligence within the helping relationship.

This book is centred on a new approach to reflection and reflective practice that emerged from research findings from a person-centred enquiry into the teaching and learning of reflection and reflective practice (Clarke 2014). The research findings produced *ten essential ingredients for successful reflection* (see Figure 1.1) and a new, extended description of reflection.

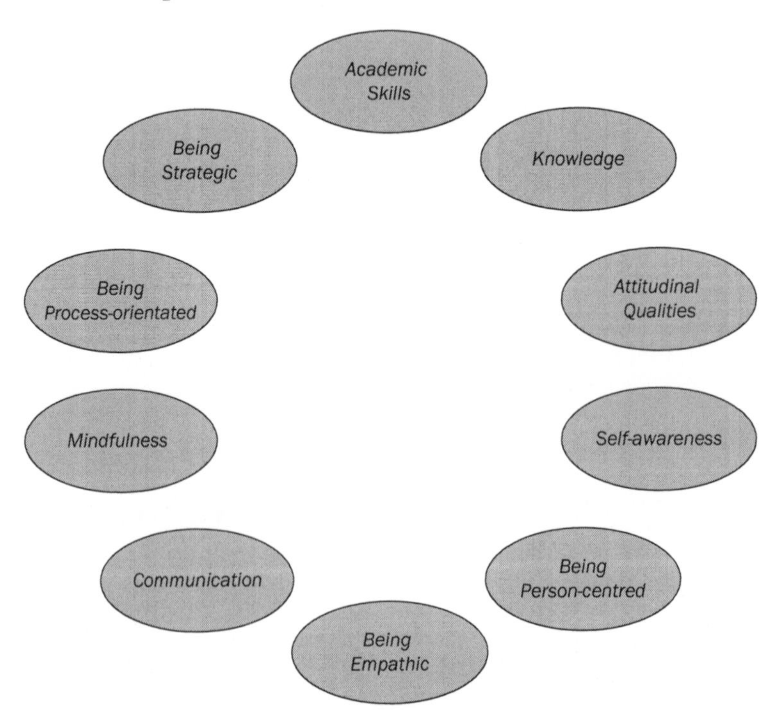


**Figure 1.1** The ten essential ingredients for successful reflection

Figure 1.1 lays out for you ten key ingredients for reflection that will be covered in the following chapters. By working your way through this book and gaining a deep understanding of what reflection is, and by utilizing these ten ingredients together, you will be able to reflect pre-, in- or on-action in any mode you choose. This may be in a written format, in quiet contemplation on your own, in the supervisory process or with a critical friend or group. These ten ingredients combined (mixed together as you would combine the ingredients for a cake) can be used independently as an approach to the way you reflect, or should you feel you need that extra structure, in combination with a reflective model or cycle that will provide you with a framework within which to reflect in whatever mode you choose. I dedicate later chapters to understanding and using some of the different reflective models and cycles, and also address how to write reflectively.

Each chapter within this book is dedicated to two of the ten essential ingredients. These ten ingredients have been paired together to show how they relate, interconnect, and support each another. A detailed explanation of each ingredient, their pairing, how you can apply them, and the benefits they can bring to your own study or practice will be explored, together with how each ingredient relates to the *new extended description* of reflection. On completion of the book, not only should you understand what reflection is, you should also have all the ingredients necessary to engage successfully and simply in the reflective process, to learn from your reflections, and to put that learning into action, thus enabling reflective practice.

But before we continue, it is important to tell you a little about how this book came about. It arose out of my own disparate experiences from student nurse to fully qualified practitioner to university lecturer. As a student nurse I was fortunate enough to have a mentor who in my final year of my mental health nursing degree not only introduced me to the complex and often misunderstood world of caring for individuals with substance misuse issues, but acted as my critical friend until the day he retired. He introduced me to the most wonderful world of reflection and reflective practice and instilled in me a lifelong learning ethos of getting to know myself. It is this ethos and engaging in the reflective process that has enabled me to be the person I am today, a person who learns from all of her experiences, a factor of utmost importance when working in the clinical field of substance misuse. I was therefore quite surprised when I started work as a senior lecturer to find that the third year students I came into contact with did not understand the concept or the importance of reflection and reflective practice. I was also perhaps even more concerned that my post-registration nurses also not only seemed to have a poor grasp of reflection, but would offer differing levels of understanding when asked to tell me what they thought reflection was. What I found most concerning was that this was occurring even though reflection is a much-discussed topic in nursing and health literature, from an educational and nursing perspective. It is not a new concept, and there appears to be consensus in the literature as to what reflection is and its function. Consequently, the purpose of this book is not to present a further theoretical discussion on reflection, thus duplicating all that is already out there on the shelf, but to offer you, the student nurse, an easy-to-read guide, a 'how to' on reflection that should support the teaching experienced by you, the student.

So, let us take a look first at what is meant by reflection.

## What is reflection?

> By three methods we may learn wisdom: First, by reflection which is noblest; second, by imitation which is easiest; and third by experience, which is the bitterest.
>
> Confucius – Chinese philosopher

For those of you who have attempted to read around the subject of reflection, you will know that there is an absolute wealth of material out there telling us what reflection is. There are authors in this field that offer good insights into reflection and reflective practice and who have written extensively. These include Melanie Jasper, Dawn Freshwater, Christopher Johns, Beverley Taylor, and Gillie Bolton to name but a few. You may also, as part of your training, have been introduced to reflective models and cycles and perhaps been advised to use these to reflect. However, it is of paramount importance that the person reflecting understands what reflection is and what the point of it is – otherwise any approach, model or cycle used to reflect will be used incorrectly, as the foundation of understanding supporting the reflective process will be missing (hence why the chapter on reflective models is towards the end of the book). For the most part, authors who have written extensively on the subject of reflection tend to agree with one another, which to the novice reflector is extremely helpful.

Have a go at the following exercise.

**Exercise 1.1: Defining reflection**

Write your own definition of reflection in the space below and then see how it compares to those that follow.

I would define reflection as:

Christopher Johns, who has written comprehensively on the subject of reflection and also produced one of the more useful reflective frameworks – and which I discuss in Chapter 5 – has described reflection as:

> . . . a window through which the practitioner can view and focus the self within the context of their lived experience in ways that enable the person to confront, understand and work towards resolving the contradictions within their practice between what is desirable and actual practice.
>
> (Johns 2000: 34)

Quite simply, Johns perceives reflection as a way of critically examining our experiences and learning from them. He views reflection as a tool that allows us to understand our practice as healthcare workers and to bridge the gap between what we do in our practice and what we *should* be doing.

Gillie Bolton (2010), who devised *through the mirror writing*, a term she coined for a specific approach to reflecting in the written format – and a method that I discuss in detail in Chapter 8 – would like us to view reflection not only as a way of critically examining and learning from our own experiences but, a more purposeful way of perceiving experiences we have from a range of viewpoints and potential scenarios. Bolton argues we can achieve this by going beyond self-indulgent ruminations and the notion that to reflect is to self-indulgently (or painfully critically) think about ourselves. Instead, we should be trying to understand how others perceived our experience. In becoming reflexive (understanding how we are affected by others and how others are affected by us), our reflection has purpose and meaning, resulting in learning and possible action (reflective practice).

> Learning and developing through examining what we think happened on any one occasion, and how we think others perceived the event and us, opening our practice to scrutiny by others, and studying data and texts from the wider sphere. It is an in-depth consideration of events or situations outside oneself: solitarily or with critical support.
>
> (Bolton 2010: 13)

John Dewey, a prominent figure in the field of education and an important proponent of reflective practice, viewed reflection as a specialized form of thinking, a key component of the process he termed *inquiry*. He described it as a form of thinking that comprises turning a subject over in the mind and giving it serious consideration. His definition of reflection is that it is:

> Active, persistent and careful consideration of any belief or supposed form of knowledge in the light of the grounds that support it, and further conclusions to which it leads . . . it includes a conscious and voluntary effort to establish belief upon a firm basis of evidence and rationality.
>
> (Dewey 1933, cited in Moon 2001: 4)

This notion of viewing reflection as an inquiry perhaps helps us to see that reflection is akin to investigation. By using terms such as *investigating or inquiring*, you may, like me, be able to conjure up an image of a detective, probing deeply into a situation we have experienced, are about to experience or are experiencing, in order to gain knowledge. Knowledge that will tell us something about ourselves, which will then inform future actions and future behaviour, and maybe even change and inform current behaviour or actions.

Reflection can be further viewed as a process in learning that can occur through thoughtful consideration of practice or experiences, allowing us to have an authentic, real voice that supports the development of awareness or a conscious knowledge with the aim of increasing our self-awareness (Ghaye 1996; Cooke and Matarasso 2005).

I would like to suggest at this point that reflection in its broadest sense means to appraise or evaluate and understand ourselves – our thoughts, feelings, and behaviours – in relation to our experiences with the intention of using that information to improve and develop cognitively (thoughtfully) and affectively (emotionally). Fundamentally, the process of and the outcome of reflection leads to the notion of change within the self, leading to heightened levels of self-awareness and therefore greater levels of emotional intelligence within the individual who is reflecting. For the most part, definitions of reflection hint at the transformational potential of reflection, and when reflection leads to change in an individual or a change in practice, it becomes reflective practice (Boyd and Fales 1983; Freshwater 1998, 2000, 2007; Jasper 2003).

Look now at the definition of reflection you provided in Exercise 1.1. Review your definition in light of what we have just discussed. Is your definition of reflection similar to any of those discussed above, or are there differences? You may find your definition is perhaps more akin to older, more mechanical, simple references to critical incident analysis where we consider how things could be avoided, overcome or improved (Hagland 1998). When I ask my students what they think reflection is, they often respond thus:

> Looking back at what happened, what went wrong, what went well, and what can we now do to make it better for future practice.

What do you think is missing here in light of what we have discussed so far? You may have recognized that the missing aspect is the added dimension of the self. Reflecting is so much more than just evaluating the mechanics of an event, incident or experience.

I suggested early on in this chapter that an extended description of reflection emerged from research previously undertaken into the teaching and learning of reflection and reflective practice. The students and staff who took part in that enquiry had quite clear ideas as to what reflection is and how they would describe it. The following is the resulting extended description of reflection from research participants' ideas and opinions combined with results from an extensive review of the literature (adapted from Clarke 2014):

### A new, extended description of reflection

'Reflection is an essential, engaging process that allows the reflector to frame and reframe their reality that is being experienced moment by moment. It requires us to utilize skills of communication, to become our own person-centred therapists, understanding ourselves in relation to experiences we are about to have, are having or have had, empathically and with accuracy, then stepping beyond the self and using this knowledge gained to understand how we may then have impacted on those around us. For this process to bear fruit, we must leave arrogance and complacency at the door, be kind and compassionate, offering ourselves unconditional positive regard, be actively engaged in mindfulness, consciously aware of the self in the moment, open to learning and sourcing new knowledge if the knowledge is not already known to us, using the new knowledge gained to develop ourselves personally and professionally in a critically analytical manner. When fully engaged in the reflective process, the experience can be humbling as we realize we are not perhaps what we assumed ourselves to be, yet also rewarding as we confirm that our best may have at that time been good enough.'

Although lengthy, hence the title of 'extended description', the research participants felt that this narrative really gives the helper or practitioner a true depiction of what reflection is. However, if you are just embarking on your nursing career and class yourself as a novice reflector, it may be a little difficult and wordy to understand initially. On reading this book, having worked your way through all the chapters, you will have a thorough understanding of what reflection is, how the ten essential ingredients support understanding of the extended description, and how they enable you to embody the reflective process. Before moving on, let's have a go at breaking down some of the ideas in the extended description to gain a fuller understanding of it.

### Exercise 1.2: Understanding the extended description

Read the extended description and consider what it is you understand about it and jot down any aspects of it you don't understand in the space below. On completing the book, return to this exercise and try to answer any queries or questions that you may have had.

Ideas from the extended description that I understand:

I need to gain a better understanding of:

Now that we have a rudimentary understanding of what reflection is, let us consider the importance of reflection.

## Why is reflection important?

The notion of reflection as a significant concept in nurse education was greatly influenced in the 1990s by a developing awareness over many years on the part of nurse educators of the need to encourage their students to become thoughtful individuals capable of critical and innovative thinking (Pierson 1998). Reflection is not a new concept. As you can see, Pierson was making reference to the importance of developing the student nurse into a critically innovative thinker in 1998 and the importance of reflection has become even more prominent since then. Within many nurse education programmes, it became an explicit requirement that students engage with the concept of reflection (Pierson 1998; Mantzoukas and Jasper 2004; Nicholl and Higgins 2004).

Not only are healthcare professionals required to adopt reflective practice both within their initial training and continuing professional development, it is also seen as a higher education transferable skill, evidence of which is required by the Quality Assurance Agency (QAA) (Mantzoukas and Jasper 2004; Tate and Sills 2004). Inclusion of critical reflection in the curricula of the health professions is also a requirement of professional and statutory bodies (Driscoll 2007). Indeed, the Nursing and Midwifery Council (NMC) stipulated that, starting from September 2011, reflection is a competence that needs to be demonstrated to be able to register as a mental health nurse for all pre-registration nursing programmes. The NMC has also further demonstrated recognition of the importance of reflection in the current revalidation procedure by requiring registered nurses to produce five accounts of when they have reflected, and have added a further element of a second registered nurse verifying those accounts.

You should be able to ascertain from the above that reflection is important – but why? The importance of reflection is rooted in anticipation that by undertaking reflection, the practitioner should be enabled to explore and experiment with areas of experience that might otherwise be difficult to access, and enable them to become thoughtful individuals capable of critical and innovative thinking. Bolton (2010) provides examples of these difficult to approach areas, including:

- What you can change in your context; how to work with what you find difficult.
- How to value the perspective of others, however different they may be to you.
- How others perceive you, and their feelings and thoughts about events.

- Why you become stressed and its impact upon your life and practice.
- How to counteract seemingly *given* social, cultural, and political structures.

These are all areas of experience that are of great importance in the caring professions, areas that advance our self-awareness and emotional intelligence, that ultimately support safe and best practice.

Taylor (2006) suggests that systematic approaches to reflection and action are needed to support more than one area of practice. The first area she suggests reflection can be of use is strengthening the resolve of nurses in order for them to be effective and happy at work. By reflecting and understanding ourselves and by being able to work though issues, we can also let things go, preventing destructive rumination.

Taylor also suggests that reflection enables us to manage the modern challenges of practice. For qualified practitioners, these modern challenges of practice include dealing with how the economic climate is affecting resources, staffing cutbacks, reductions in the numbers of trainee nursing posts commissioned, too many patients, too few beds, and so on.

Further challenges that are the crux of the caring profession include supporting vulnerable people, helping people with challenging behaviour, coping with others' mental distress, high turnover of staff on wards, and accepting the potential for possible physical or verbal attack/abuse on the part of those being cared for. Bolton (2010) agrees with Taylor and suggests that reflection and reflexivity are essential for responsible and ethical practice, and enabling us as practitioners to maintain our own good mental health.

It might therefore be suggested that we need reflection in our lives to:

- keep us safe;
- heighten our understanding of ourselves;
- enable self-awareness to develop;
- use the learning from reflection to support the therapeutic relationship;
- enable those we care for to achieve their own goals.

In the words of Beckett (1969: 169):

> To be capable of helping others to become all they are capable of becoming we must first fulfil that commitment to ourselves.

In a profession where evidence-based practice is the norm and where nurses strive to develop their own body of research, reflection also helps us to identify gaps in our knowledge, recognize where we need to source new knowledge, and bridge the 'theory–practice gap'. This is a term you will undoubtedly hear an awful lot of throughout your training.

Ghaye (1996) describes four purposes of reflection:

1. Linking the knowledge we already possess to thoughtful actions or practice, and from our practice experience linking what is known and what has occurred to new knowledge generated.
2. Enhancing and enriching practice and action. By allowing the reflective practitioner to discuss their experiences and their practice, different perspectives can be sought and different ways of working attempted.
3. Increasing individual and collective accountability.
4. Providing a forum within which the existing situation or current practice can be questioned in a critically constructive and supportive manner.

In just four points, Ghaye (1996) nicely sums up some of the purposes of reflection as it relates to our clinical practice. However, as you shall see throughout this book, there is another purpose that we have already alluded to, and that is the development of our self-awareness, which not only will have a positive impact on practice but also on our personal lives too.

Let us take a look, then, at when and how we reflect.

## When and how do we reflect?

Have a go at the following exercise.

## Exercise 1.3: When do we reflect?

In the space below, jot down when you think you reflect.

I reflect when:

Donald Schön is an influential thinker in developing the theory and practice of reflective learning. He divides the reflecting process into two main kinds: reflecting in-action (while you are experiencing something) and reflecting on-action (after the experience) (Schön 1983). These he describes as the principal processes professionals can use to help them uncover and articulate their knowledge. He emphasizes the idea that reflection is a way professionals can bridge the theory–practice gap as we have previously acknowledged, based on the potential of reflection to uncover knowledge both during the activity and afterwards through analysis of activity. In the nurse education setting, this should enable students to make the link between the theoretical underpinnings of nursing that are taught in the classroom and how they are applied in the clinical setting. This analysis becomes more than just reflection and can be viewed as reflective practice.

Reflection-in-action is the process by which the practitioner recognizes a new situation or a problem and thinks about it while still acting or behaving (Palmer et al. 2000). Schön (1987) and Boud and Walker (1990, cited in Smith 1998) believe that it is possible to encourage reflection-in-action and in doing so improve our ability to identify problems as they occur in real time.

Reflection-in-action is often seen as an automatic activity that occurs subconsciously. It is often perceived as an intuitive and unconscious process (Jasper 2003). 'Thinking on your feet', 'keeping your wits about you', and 'learning by doing' are everyday phrases that Schön (1983) cites to describe in real terms 'reflection-in-action'. Reflection-in-action assumes a mindful practitioner (more on mindfulness in Chapter 5) who can think at the same time as doing, and who has a knowledge base that moment-by-moment action and behaviour can be judged against. This would suggest that perhaps reflection-in-action is not undertaken subconsciously but consciously and that we are active agents in the conscious process of reflecting in-action. This may well be difficult for student nurses who are still engaged in the early learning process and do not necessarily have a full understanding of the theory behind the actions they are taking.

I would suggest that, if you view yourself as a novice reflector, you will find it easier if you first reflect 'on-action'. Reflecting 'on-action' is a little easier, as in this process you can take your time. You can have your experiences and then you can reflect when it is convenient to do so and there is no rush. And you can choose to find a person to reflect with if you feel the need to be supported and guided.

When we reflect on-action, we are able to speculate upon how a situation might have been handled differently and what other knowledge would have come in useful (Palmer et al. 2000). Jasper (2003) suggests that reflection-on-action involves us consciously exploring our experiences, analysing, investigating and thinking about practice or the experience after it has occurred. In taking our time to reflect on experiences, we may be able to view them from different perspectives to provide ourselves with more knowledge of what occurred.

Jasper (2003) has suggested that reflection-on-action can be seen as an active process of transforming your experience into knowledge and is a more complex process than simply thinking about and describing an event. Having a person who can act as your guide and critical friend will support the analysis of your experience and will help prevent the need to be too descriptive, so that thinking and practice can move forward.

It must not be forgotten that we can also reflect before an experience. It can be rewarding to apply thoughtful consideration when engaging in new experiences. This is especially useful if we are entering into unknown territory, as reflecting before-action can support us in filling the gaps in our knowledge prior to an experience.

Thus it can be said that we can reflect:

- before or pre-action;
- at the time or in-action; and
- after an experience or on-action.

Now a brief word about reflective frameworks, models, and cycles.

### Exercise 1.4: Frameworks, models, and cycles: what are they?

In the space below, make a note of what you think reflective frameworks are.

I understand the term 'reflective framework' to mean:

The terms framework, model, and cycle are often used interchangeably. Simply put, they are all tools you can use to structure the process of reflection. When reading around the literature on reflection, you will notice that various supporters have devised and advocated a range of models to guide and develop the practice of reflection-on-action. Key proponents of models for reflection and learning include Borton (1970), Boud et al. (1985), Gibbs (1988), Atkins and Murphy (1994), and Johns (2004). Though not an exhaustive list, these models are particularly popular with students and educators. These frameworks for reflection will be discussed in greater detail in Chapter 7 and I am sure that most of you will be familiar with one or more of them.

Within the university setting, it is often the case that the mode of reflection for nursing students is enforced upon them by the academic requirements of the programme and they are expected to reflect via a presentation and/or written assignments. You will in general be expected to reflect alone when writing your reflective assignments or preparing for reflective presentations and your only guide or support in the reflective process will be a reflective model or cycle – in fact, it is often a requirement of the assignment itself to use a framework, model or cycle. Although reflective practice should not be limited to this kind of assignment, these models or cycles do however provide the student nurse or reflector with a framework within which to reflect – which will be demonstrated in Chapter 7. To a certain extent, they enable a strategic approach to what could be a rather random exercise, which is very useful for the novice reflector.

However, there is a note of caution on the use of reflective models or cycles by the novice or even experienced reflector: the terminology may not be overly helpful in the development of reflective skills and in aiding the complex conversation we need to have with ourselves during the reflective process. Heath (1998) suggested that using a model of reflection at the outset might produce uniformity and suppress creativity and thinking. Models and cycles are also of little use if you do not understand what reflection is and what the point of it is, something I highlight again later in the book. I have sat in many reflective presentations and marked many reflective assignments that have received poor marks or failed because the student clearly didn't understand what it means to reflect and so used the reflective model or cycle incorrectly.

A simple tip before choosing the reflective model or cycle is to make sure you understand what it means to reflect first. By using the extended description provided here and working your way through the chapters in this book, you will be able to reflect without the use of a model or cycle, and you will be able to reflect pre-, in- or on-action. However, should you still feel you need a structure, then just combine the ingredients detailed in the following chapters with a framework, model or reflective cycle of your choice.

The next five chapters will guide you through the ingredients required for successful reflection and demonstrate to you how each ingredient is used during the different times when we reflect – ensuring that whether you are a novice or experienced reflector, you will advance your reflective skills to become effective reflective practitioners.

**Key points that can be taken from this chapter are:**

- Reflection is a process-orientated practice that allows the reflector to gain heightened levels of self-awareness, supporting the development of emotional intelligence.
- Reflection enables us to recognize our current knowledge while highlighting theoretical gaps.
- Reflection helps us to become critically analytical thinkers, able to truly evaluate experiences and as a result choose to change practice and personal behaviours.
- Reflection enables us to view our experiences from different perspectives while recognizing how we are impacted upon by others, and how we impact on those around us.
- Reflection can occur at any time.
- Changing our experiences moment by moment, or applying the learning taken from reflection-in-action, becomes reflective practice.

CHAPTER

# 2 Academic skills and knowledge

## Essential ingredient #1 – *Academic skills*

*'Reflecting is not a vivid description of an event, a situation or an experience, but a review of the experience prior to, during or after, in a critically analytical manner. This critical analysis must be supported by knowledge, particularly knowledge that can bridge the theory–practice gap and so be meaningful to practice experience. New knowledge gained is then amalgamated with the old and current knowledge, from which the person can then synthesize a new way of being, or expand and enhance the current way of being.'*

(Adapted from Clarke 2014)

## Essential ingredient #2 – *Knowledge*

*'The practitioner, in order to evaluate and reflect upon what they are experiencing in the clinical setting, needs to have a level of knowledge that they can refer to and evaluate their experience against. If they do not have the existing knowledge, they need to know how to source the knowledge so that they may bridge that theory–practice gap, and enhance their ability to understand the experience they are reflecting on, prior to, in action or on action.'*

(Adapted from Clarke 2014)

## Learning outcomes

By the end of this chapter, you will be able to:

- Understand how academic skills support the reflective process
- Demonstrate understanding of the difference between descriptive reflection and reflection that is critically analytical
- Demonstrate understanding of the part knowledge plays in the reflective process
- Understand why reflection supports the development of self-awareness and the gaining of new knowledge
- Understand the concepts of reflection and reflective practice.

## Introduction

The aim of this chapter is to highlight the difference between descriptive reflection and analytical reflection and to highlight the roles that knowledge and the academic skills of critique and analysis play in supporting the critically reflective process. Nurses not only need to be caring, compassionate, and kind but also need to be able to work within an evidence-based framework, possessing the cognitive skills of decision-making and problem-solving (Wilkinson 1996). Being able to critically review literature, research, and clinical guidelines ensures safe and effective practice (Atkins 2004; Taylor 2006).

## Academic skills

Let's take a look at our first essential ingredient – academic skills.

### Essential ingredient #1 – *Academic skills*

*'Reflecting is not a vivid description of an event, a situation or an experience, but a review of the experience prior to, during or after, in a critically analytical manner. This critical analysis must be supported by knowledge, particularly knowledge that can bridge the theory-practice gap and so be meaningful to practice experience.*

*New knowledge gained is then amalgamated with the old and current knowledge, from which the person can then synthesize a new way of being, or expand and enhance the current way of being.'*

(Adapted from Clarke 2014)

When I teach academic skills and critical analysis to undergraduate nurses and seasoned healthcare practitioners, I always ask about previous experiences of academic writing and the response is often:

'My feedback tells me I am too descriptive.'

I then ask about the role of critical analysis in academic writing and the response tends to be silence! Or:

'I don't know how to be analytical.'

To generate understanding, I ask my students to reflect on their roles at work in the clinical area, or on life in general in relation to the decisions they make. I ask them to consider the decision-making process and I ask them to take me step by step through what they would do in order to make a fully informed choice. What I highlight during the discussion is where they are being analytical and where critique has occurred. What usually occurs is what is often referred to as a 'light bulb moment'. At this point, a student is able to associate and recognize the mental agility that they employ in everyday life as a transferable skill to academia. Critical analysis becomes somewhat less of a mystery (you will come across examples of everyday life in terms of the skills of critique and analysis later in the chapter).

However, this newfound understanding is not always then transferred to reflection and reflective writing. When using reflective models to structure one's reflections, especially in relation to reflective writing and presentations, it unfortunately becomes common practice for some students to provide beautiful lengthy descriptions of the experience they are reflecting upon with wonderful descriptive references to how the experience made them feel. It is not uncommon for students to say to me:

'Reflective writing is easy as it's not very academic.'

Or:

'Why do I need to use literature and analysis when I am writing about myself?'

Research conducted highlighted very clearly that students were not being taught the true meaning of reflection and how the reflective process is underpinned by all the principal academic skills (Clarke 2014). From my own observations of teaching reflection across all programmes in a faculty of health, I am acutely aware of lecturers' differing frame of reference in relation to reflection and the confusion – as discussed in the previous chapter – between their understanding of the reflective process and mechanical critical incident analysis. Let us consider critical incident analysis for a moment to briefly clarify why I feel it is slightly different to that of reflection. Have a look at the following example of an experience/incident:

**Giving an injection**

An experienced female nurse has given an injection to a service user/patient using a new evidenced-based technique that the nurse has not used before. The giving of the injection does not go smoothly, and it takes a number of attempts before it is given correctly. As a result, the service user/patient is quite distressed and the injection hurt more than it should have.

If this incident was addressed using critical incident analysis, the nurse might first consider what she thought went wrong and maybe what went well. She would refer to and review the evidence, literature, and guidance on how to perform the new injection technique. New knowledge would be gained, old correct knowledge affirmed, and old incorrect knowledge rejected, allowing the nurse to determine what actually went wrong and what would need to happen next time.

However, at no point has the nurse analysed her actual thoughts and feelings, or tried to understand her behaviour during this experience. Why would an experienced nurse give an injection using a new technique without first reviewing and checking the evidence and guidance for that technique? What thoughts and feelings did the nurse have at the time? Why did she think and feel this way? Why did she act and behave in this manner? What impact did she think she had upon the service user/patient? What impact did the environment and patient have on the nurse? These are the sorts of questions (Socratic questions that assume not to know) that would be raised during reflection and which I perceive to be the difference between reflection and critical incident analysis.

There is also a fundamental issue with the way in which critical analysis is often taught. It is common for students to be taught critical analysis with the emphasis on the critique of simply acknowledging pros and cons (this may ring a bell with you), without any focus on the most important aspect of critical analysis – the *analysis*. If analysis is not understood and then engaged with, the critique will remain descriptive.

If we take a brief look at two widely used reflective models – Gibbs' (1988) reflective cycle and Borton's (1970) framework for guiding reflective activities – we can see that both models require the person reflecting to provide a description of the event (see Figures 2.1 and 2.2).

In the case of Gibbs (1988), immersing ourselves in the experience so we can provide a description of the event and then recalling thoughts, feelings, and behaviours is required. In the case of Borton (1970), the 'What?' requires us to tell the story of what happened. The problem occurs when the person reflecting becomes consumed with the need to describe at length what happened – then, at length, the feelings that were experienced. This is further hindered when you are advised as students to use reflective models as assignment structures for reflective writing, rather than frameworks to guide the reflective process. A lengthy description of the experience and the feelings that arose is then presumed to be reflecting, but at this

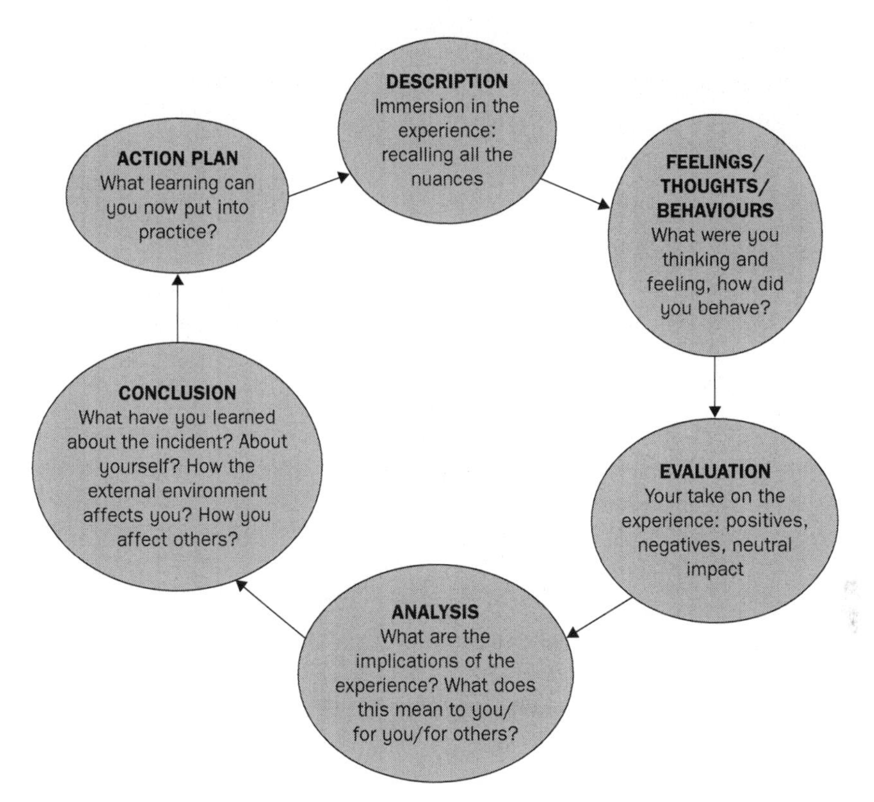


**Figure 2.1** Gibbs' reflective cycle
Source: Adapted from Gibbs (1988).

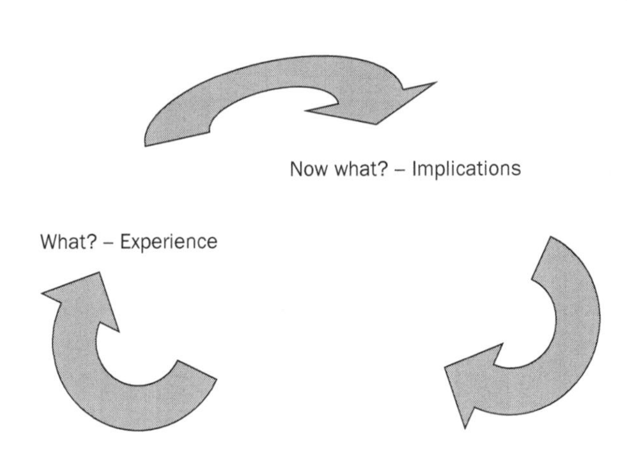


**Figure 2.2** Borton's reflective framework
Source: Adapted from Borton (1970).

point no meaningful learning has occurred and the lengthy description of what took place becomes just a story. If you refer to feedback you received on written reflective assignments, it may have suggested that you were 'too descriptive for this level'.

In order to ensure that our recollection of events and description of experiences is not just a vivid retelling of a story, it is important that we apply the same academic skills that we apply to normal academic practices to our reflection also. To learn from the description, we have to understand both the description and its deeper meaning. In essence, we need to apply the concept of critical analysis to the description of the experience. At the end of the day, what we are trying to achieve in the reflective process is a greater self-awareness, to support the development of emotional intelligence and ultimately transformational change within ourselves and/or our practice, should change be appropriate.

*Scenario 2.1*

The following is a snapshot of a female student's reflective writing. This student was undertaking a module in substance misuse. The assessed element of the module requires the student to give up a behaviour for one week, reflect upon the experience, and use the learning gained from the reflective process to help enhance her understanding of substance misuse, which she can then apply to her practice. The student decided to give up wearing makeup.

> The word abstinence made me feel nervous. I associated abstinence with refraining from drugs or alcohol, so the fact I was now giving up makeup – was that telling me that perhaps I had a subconscious addiction to wearing makeup. I had told my husband and daughters and they wondered why I was so anxious and what the fuss was all about. I had reinforced negative automatic thoughts about people staring at me and talking about me. I felt my heart raced when I thought about it and I felt embarrassed that I was getting myself worked up over makeup when there are so many more important things to worry about. I kept making excuses not to start. There was always an obstacle such as a planned event. I would plan and say 'start tomorrow' and then I would have an attack of nerves. The planning and preparing took much longer than I anticipated. I was also mindful that time was

going by and I had to do it sooner rather than later to allow time for me to write my reflective journal. I was not prepared for the feelings that I was to experience. They were almost like having withdrawal symptoms. I have been makeup free before, so I didn't understand why this was different. Without sounding like a drama queen, I felt traumatized. I didn't like being told I had to give something up.

**Exercise 2.1: Review of the two reflective models**

- What elements of Gibbs' cycle and Borton's framework do you think have been used here?
- What learning do you think has occurred here?
- Has self-awareness been enhanced?

You probably realize that this student has got stuck in the descriptive phase of each of the models – the description and feelings stages in Gibbs' cycle, the 'What?' stage in Borton's framework. You should also be able to see the descriptive nature of this snapshot where only surface level learning is taking place. Later, you will see a snapshot of a different student's work for the same assignment that incorporates the aspects of critique and analysis.

## So, what is critical analysis?

In order to undertake critical analysis, we must first understand what it means to think in a critical manner. Critical thinkers in nursing have been described as truth seekers, demonstrating open-mindedness, suspending judgement, having an intellectual curiosity that allows them to seek answers to questions about themselves and their practice (Paul 1993). A student or nurse who thinks critically about what they have experienced, or are experiencing, sees beyond the surface of what is occurring and seeks answers in an attempt to understand what is occurring. To think critically, we need to remember, gather information, accumulate evidence, understand our own assumptions and beliefs about the experience, draw on current knowledge, recognize and fill the gaps in our knowledge, analyse, and ultimately draw conclusions. A critical thinker doesn't just see the trees; they get lost in the wood, and will question each turn and review each path and its implications before emerging on the other side.

During the critical thinking process, the student or nurse will analyse the information that their intellectual curiosity is bringing to their conscious mind. To be critical of the information, they will acknowledge the material and break it down into its fundamental parts, before determining how the parts are related to each other and to an overall structure (Mayer 2002).

*Scenario 2.2*

The following scenario is a snapshot of another student's reflective writing for the same assignment brief as Scenario 2.1. This piece of reflection demonstrates some of the principles of analysis. This male student decided to give up tea and coffee.

With this in mind I decided to spend a couple of days thinking about what I get from tea and coffee before trying to stop again. What I found during this pre-contemplation exploration was that I have an almost constant mild craving for tea or coffee throughout the whole day and that it is this craving that was driving my mindless behaviour to put the kettle on, sometimes without me being fully aware of it. But what exactly was I craving? This seemed to be the central question. If I could identify this, then I would have something real to work with. When I explored this craving more closely, I discovered that I found comfort in two qualities that are present in both tea and coffee. The first is the warmth of the drink. And the second is the sweetness of the drink. To my surprise I found that, other than these two qualities, I did not really like anything else about tea or coffee. That said, the idea of drinking hot sweet water has no appeal, which suggests that there is something else in tea and coffee that I find desirable (maybe the caffeine itself?). This was both interesting and helpful, but I still needed to better understand why I craved these qualities of warmth and sweetness. After observing my own behaviour, and considering this for quite some time, I came to the conclusion that I was using the comfort that I found in these drinks as a means of managing my emotions. More precisely, I was using tea and coffee as an aversion strategy for anxiety and boredom – two emotions that have played a big part in my life.

Can you see the difference between this piece of reflective writing and that in Scenario 2.1? Try to identify explicit differences in the writing between the student who abstained from tea and coffee and that of the student who abstained from wearing makeup.

You should be able to see how the second student has engaged with analytical and critical thinking and the difference it has made to his writing and recollection of his experience. We will return to this later to compare the two pieces of writing and pinpoint where critical analysis takes place.

Now take a look at Figure 2.3, which demonstrates how a simple topic such as a 'film review' can be broken down into its component parts (similar to mind mapping) in order to analyse the impact of the connections between the parts, and as a consequence understand how the connections impact upon the topic of a film review.

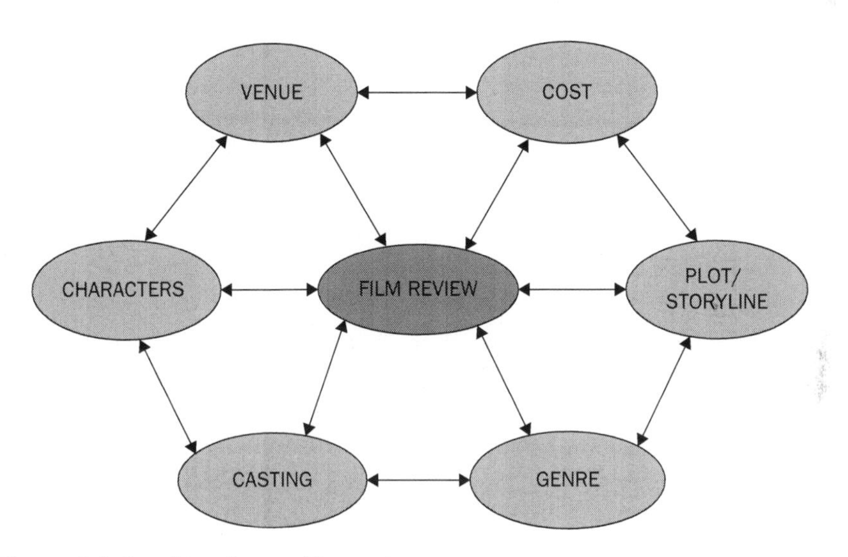


**Figure 2.3** Breaking down a film review

Here, the topic of a film review has been broken down into parts that might be considered to reflect a good film. If I were to tell a friend about a film I had seen, these are the aspects I would likely discuss (not dissimilar to being a film critic). In order to now critically analyse how these parts relate to the topic, we apply intellectual curiosity to each of the parts and ask questions that help us to understand what it is about each part that helps in the process of reviewing a film. The next step is to apply intellectual curiosity to each part and question how they relate to and impact upon one another, and then question how the answers contribute to an overall impact upon the topic. As we do this, we can see that critique and analysis become interchangeable and most often analysis will take place before critique.

## Exercise 2.2: Film review

Imagine you are with a friend and you are telling them about a film you have seen. Have a go at breaking down the topic of a film review into its component parts. Ask 'what?' and 'why?' questions of each of the parts. For example: What is it about a particular part that can help you to review the film you have seen? What are the implications of that part to the topic? Then ask yourself how all the parts relate to and impact upon one another, and how the new knowledge gained from this analysis contributes to the overall impact on your film review.

Note that the topic chosen can be anything from a good day out to a favourite meal or a favourite place. What is important at this point is the process of breaking information down.

Eventually through this process you will be able to recognize the knowledge you have, while also gaining new knowledge about yourself in relation to the topic you have chosen. What we are trying to achieve here is meaningful learning. That is, we are seeking to make sense of experiences. On making sense of what we already know (old knowledge), we gain new knowledge that can be merged with the old knowledge, which can then be used to make a transformational change within our self and/or to our practice – we become more emotionally intelligent. This is often referred to as bridging the theory–practice gap.

Having attempted this exercise, you should not only recognize which factors affect a film, you will also have a deep understanding of why certain factors are important to your film review. This knowledge will raise your self-awareness and will aid you in the future when deciding whether to view a film.

## Knowledge

Let's take a look at our second essential ingredient – knowledge.

### Essential ingredient #2 – *Knowledge*

*'The practitioner, in order to evaluate and reflect upon what they are experiencing in the clinical setting, needs to have a level of knowledge that they can refer to and evaluate their experience against. If they do not have the existing knowledge, they need to know how to source the knowledge so that they may bridge that theory-practice gap, and enhance their ability to understand the experience they are reflecting on, prior to, in action or on action.'*

(Adapted from Clarke 2014)

We will now focus on how the reflective, critically analytical process can be supported when you are engaged in university academic activities, by seeking out and gaining new knowledge.

When you write an academic discursive essay, or are required to undertake a presentation, you will know that your arguments, statements, discussions, and opinions must be supported and created by evidence from the literature to give credibility to the debate. However, you will also need to demonstrate you have engaged in meaningful research on a particular topic and that you can understand what you have been reading. What is interesting is that many of my students think that the research skills they have acquired, including the ability to use the literature appropriately to create academic pieces of work, are not necessary when reflecting. As I noted previously, my students often say to me:

'Reflection is about me and it's personal, so why do I need to research as well?'

In answer to this question, it is just as important to use these skills when reflecting. Evidence and literature can enhance the understanding we gain from our experiences, can help determine whether our current knowledge is correct or needs to be refined, as well as help identify those gaps in our knowledge that we are not aware of. It can help us determine if our tacit (assumed) knowledge is correct, current, and relevant, and it can support a critique and analysis of what we already know. The research knowledge you gain will help you raise questions about yourself, your practice, and your learning.

In Scenario 2.3, you will see how research knowledge comes into play to help the student to better understand her experience through reflection. The enhanced understanding obtained by applying the evidence base and the increased knowledge gained can then be applied to clinical practice, enabling reflective practice.

### *Scenario 2.3*

This scenario is a snapshot of the reflective writing of the same student as in Scenario 2.2. This piece of reflection demonstrates the principles of reflection underpinned by use of the literature to enhance the reflective process. The knowledge gained allowed the student to enhance his understanding of caring for people with an addictive disorder.

> On finishing that cup of tea I began to feel a little uncomfortable. I started to think that perhaps abstaining from tea and coffee was not going to be as easy as I had thought. Critical thoughts about my inability to control myself also started to arise. In turn, this generated negative emotional feelings that I would normally associate with low mood, in my body. At first this failure seemed to me to be nothing more than a setback, a delay in my progress, a possible weakness in my character. However, when I thought about it some more I started to think that there might be an important lesson to be learned from this initial 'failure' that might help me better understand substance misuse and abstinence. When I researched this I found that what I had been experiencing was 'ambivalence', which, according to a school of counselling called motivational interviewing, is understood to be a central obstacle to change (Miller and Rollnick 2002). Another relevant set of ideas that I came across while researching this is Prochaska and DiClimente's cycle of change, which is made up of six stages, including a pre-contemplation stage, in which a person has not started to think that

there could be any problem associated with their behaviour and may not be experiencing any. Looking back it seems that this 'failure' represents the first important lesson that I learned as a result of this exercise. I now understand this lesson in the following terms – failure to abstain should not be understood as failure, but rather as an indicator of the presence of ambivalence in the mind of the abstainer, which may be rooted in a lack of preparation at the pre-contemplation stage.

### Exercise 2.3: What is the difference?

Take another look at the first snapshot of reflective writing, in Scenario 2.1 (giving up wearing makeup). Note down the differences between this scenario and Scenario 2.3 (giving up tea and coffee). Try using precise words, sentences, and questions to illustrate your points, so you can reflect on how you might use these techniques yourself to become more critical.

- Which scenario is descriptive?
- Which uses the literature?
- Which is analytical?
- Which enhances self-awareness?

The second student not only explained how he felt, but also asked himself why he felt that way. Note that he asked himself a lot of probing questions in order to seek answers. He observed his own behaviour and asked himself why it follows certain patterns. He then broke down the elements of the tea-making process and the drink itself to identify the component parts and to examine what value each holds for him. Only by doing this was he able to draw any conclusions.

## Process

So how do we do this when reflecting? How are the ingredients of academic skills and knowledge (critical analysis, knowledge/research) executed as part of the reflective process? Have a look at the following scenario to see these ingredients in action.

*Scenario 2.4*

You are a second-year student nurse and your mentor asks you to formulate a person-centred care plan with a service user you have been spending time with during your clinical placement. Your mentor wants to assess your person-centred care planning skills.

Boxes 2.1, 2.2, and 2.3 provide examples of how old and new knowledge can be utilized as part of the three different modes of reflection and how critical analysis plays a role in meaningful learning.

## Box 2.1: Reflection pre-action

**Stage 1** – Drawing on current **knowledge** of this service user, **reflect** by recalling what you think you know about them to this point. Consider why you know this and how you know this. Then consider your thoughts and feelings about what you know and **analyse** why you currently think and feel the way you do about this person and how you feel about undertaking the care planning session. At this point, you are reflecting pre-action in a **critically analytical** manner drawing on old and current **knowledge**.

**Stage 2** – Consider your current **knowledge** of care planning.

**Stage 3** – Again using the skills of **critical analysis**, ask questions of your current **knowledge** in relation to the task at hand, in order to identify gaps in current **knowledge**. For example:

- Do you know how to practically undertake care planning?
- Do you know what a person-centred care plan is?
- Do you know how to be person-centred?
- Do you have person-centred knowledge of the service user?
- Do you know what the person-centred needs of the service user are?
- Do you understand why you think and feel the way you do about this experience?

**Stage 4** – Gaining new **knowledge**. Take action to fill the gaps in current knowledge, i.e.

- Research care planning
- Speak to mentor
- Observe mentor

- Meet with the service user – get to know them
- Research the person-centred approach
- Research person-centred care planning
- Practise person-centred communication skills and reflect with your mentor on your progress.

**Stage 5** – Acknowledge and compare new **knowledge** gained with old **knowledge**. You understand that the new **knowledge** either supersedes the old **knowledge** or can be assimilated and utilized harmoniously with it. At this point, a **transformational change** might take place.

**Stage 6** – Consider, process, and **analyse** the information amassed to carry out the task requested of you.

## Box 2.2: Reflection-in-action

**Stage 1** – Begins in the moment you walk into the room and undertake the person-centred care plan with the service user. You **reflect** by becoming mindful of your thoughts, feelings, and behaviour.

**Stage 2** – While engaging in the task requested of you, continue to **reflect** by being fully aware of your thoughts, feelings, and behaviour moment to moment. Also **analyse** the way you think, feel, and behave by observing your service user's responses to you and constantly checking yourself against their responses, being mindful.

**Stage 3** – As you **reflect** in-action, you will realize you have some **knowledge** because you will be recalling in the moment information you need to support your engagement with the service user: you know small amounts of information about the service user, what a care plan should look like, you have likely seen a care planning session carried out by your mentor, and you know how to ask questions.

**Stage 4** – It is also at this point you realize you may not have enough **knowledge**. You may possess superficial information about the service user from a person-centred perspective. You may have very little **knowledge** about person-centred care planning and the person-centred approach. You may also consider at this point why you chose not to recognize gaps in your **knowledge** prior to engaging in this experience – **analysis**.

**Stage 5** – Carry out the formulation of the care plan even when recognizing that there are fundamental gaps in your **knowledge.** But acknowledge the gaps and log this for future reference. Acknowledge how the gaps in **knowledge** have made you feel and how it has impacted on your ability to carry out the task and as a result how it has affected your engagement with the service user.

**Stage 6** – Following the experience, **reflect** and recall the gaps in your **knowledge** and take steps to fill them. Contemplate more deeply why there were gaps, why these gaps were not filled prior to the experience, and how engaging in the task with these gaps in **knowledge** felt for you, and felt for the service user – **analysis and critique**.

**Stage 7** – Acknowledge and compare new **knowledge** gained with old **knowledge**. You understand that the new **knowledge** either supersedes the old **knowledge** or can be assimilated and utilized harmoniously with it.

**Stage 8** – **Reflect** by considering what you have learned about yourself in this process and what this experience has taught you in relation to your personal and professional development – **analysis** and raising self-awareness. At this point, a **transformational change** might take place.

## Box 2.3: Reflection-on-action

**Stage 1** – Having undertaken the person-centred care plan and having had the experience, either alone or with a friend, colleague, your mentor, personal tutor or as part of a group, **reflect** by thinking about or discussing the event in detail. This is a **reflective** conversation. Your **reflective** discussion will focus upon understanding your experience from your own point of view and from the point of view of the others involved, i.e. being **reflexive**. How do you rate your performance on the task? What were your thoughts, feelings, behaviour, how do you think the service user felt? Ask 'why' and 'what' questions of what you thought/felt/behaved. Discuss or contemplate the implications of those thoughts, feelings, and behaviours – **analysis**. At this point, you will have gained new **knowledge** about yourself in the context of this experience.

**Stage 2** – Discuss what it is you already know about person-centred care planning – **knowledge**.

**Stage 3** – Stages 1 and 2 will provide the framework that will support recognition that there may have been aspects of the care planning process that did not go as well as expected. Recognize that this could be because there are gaps in your current **knowledge** that hindered your ability to carry out the task in full, or engendered a lack of confidence within yourself.

**Stage 4** – Acknowledge the gaps in your **knowledge** and take steps to fill them – **research**.

**Stage 5** – Acknowledge and compare new **knowledge** gained with old **knowledge**. You understand that the new **knowledge** either supersedes the old **knowledge** or can be assimilated and utilized harmoniously with it.

**Stage 6** – Reflect further by considering what you have learned about yourself in this process and what this experience has taught you in relation to your personal and professional development – **analysis.** At this point, a **transformational change** might take place.

## Exercise 2.4: Now have a go!

| *Reflection pre-action* | *Reflection-in-action* | *Reflection-on-action* |
|---|---|---|
| The next time you are asked to experience something that is new to you, reflect and think about the following:<br>• What do you currently know regarding the experience you are about to have?<br>• Do you have the full **knowledge**?<br>• Are there gaps in your **knowledge**?<br>• If there are gaps, fill them – **research** | The next time you experience something on clinical placement or within the university setting (e.g. in role-play, making a cup of tea with a service user), in the moment reflect and consider:<br>• What do you already **know** about what you are currently experiencing?<br>• What do you not **know** about what you are currently experiencing? | The next time you have an experience on clinical placement or within the university setting, reflect and consider:<br>• What was the experience like for me?<br>• What did I think and feel?<br>• Why do I think I felt and thought in that way?<br>• What was happening for me at the time to engender these thoughts and feelings?<br>• How did I behave? |

| *Reflection pre-action* | *Reflection-in-action* | *Reflection-on-action* |
|---|---|---|
| • Are you confident in your ability to engage in this experience?<br>• What are your preconceived ideas about this experience?<br>• Will this experience tell you anything about yourself that you don't already know?<br>• Where do you think these ideas and beliefs originate from and what do they mean to you?<br>• Think about the new **knowledge** gained – can it work harmoniously with your existing **knowledge**, or does it supersede current **knowledge**?<br>Now have the experience and think about what it might have been like had you not filled in those gaps | • Is there a framework within which you could underpin the work you are doing with a service user?<br>• Is this experience teaching you anything about yourself?<br>• Are your thoughts, feelings, and behaviours impacting upon you or the service user in a positive or negative way?<br>• Has the experience highlighted any gaps in your **knowledge** that need filling?<br>Following the experience, fill in those gaps in your knowledge and contemplate the same event had those gaps in your knowledge been filled. Would the experience have been different? | • Why did I behave in this manner?<br>• What impact did I have on those around me?<br>• Has this experience highlighted any gaps in my **knowledge?**<br>• What has this experience taught me about myself?<br>Now consider the gaps in your **knowledge** and fill them. Filling in the gaps might enable future similar events to be experienced more as you would like them to |

**In all three cases, ask yourself 'what do I know about myself?'**

It was the intention of this chapter to demonstrate how the two ingredients of **academic skills** and **knowledge** play a vital role in the reflective process. How, by engaging in the reflective process and combining these ingredients, there is potential for you as the reflector to ultimately use the knowledge gained from reflection to generate a positive change within yourself and/or in your practice – transformational change. If we revisit the extended description of reflection, we can see where these two ingredients are situated:

> . . . open to learning and sourcing new knowledge if the knowledge is not already known to us, using the new knowledge gained to develop ourselves personally and professionally in a critically analytical manner.

**Key points that can be taken from this chapter are:**

- Academic skills play a key role in the critically reflective process.
- Critical analysis is a concept that can be applied to everyday life situations and is a transferable skill.
- The role of critical analysis in the reflective process is to provide meaning to the description of an experience to ensure deeper levels of learning.
- Academic skills are not just useful in analysing a critical incident, they also support the gaining of self-awareness in the reflective process and enhancement of emotional intelligence.
- Knowledge old and new plays a vital role in supporting the learning that takes place when reflecting.
- Reflecting is a mode that can highlight gaps in your knowledge.
- Research plays a key part in the reflective process to support the learning that can occur.
- Reflection can lead to transformational change within the reflector.

CHAPTER

# Attitudinal qualities and self-awareness

## Essential ingredient #3 – *Attitudinal qualities*

*'The driving force of successful engagement with the reflective process. The practitioner needs to be humble to the process, be open, honest, and willing, having the motivation to understand and learn. The practitioner needs to be brave, courageous, and confident in order to encourage the honesty required in the process. Kindness, compassion, and offering unconditional positive regard to oneself enable openness.'*

(Adapted from Clarke 2014)

## Essential ingredient #4 – *Self-awareness*

*'The practitioner needs to have a current level of awareness of self, a perception of how they perceive themselves to be. It is this current knowledge of self that is the basis for the reflective process. Self-awareness allows the individual to be honest about how they perceive themselves to "be" in the experience. It is this existing knowledge of the self that is also agreed, challenged, developed, and overturned, in and by, the reflective process.'*

(Adapted from Clarke 2014)

## Learning outcomes

By the end of this chapter, you will be able to:

- Understand the importance of, and demonstrate an understanding of, the attitudinal qualities and how they support successful reflection
- Determine how connected you are with these qualities and be able to recognize areas for enhancement
- Understand the notion of self-awareness and the vital role it plays in reflective practice.
- Use some of the hints and tips within this chapter to start the process of developing greater levels of self-awareness within you.

In Chapter 2, we addressed the important role *academic skills* and *knowledge* play in the reflective process. We took a detailed look at these terms and their relationship with reflection. However, as we can see from the extended description of reflection given in Chapter 1, reflection is multidimensional with the added characteristic of using ourselves/me/you in the reflective process to learn not just about an event or experience, but to learn about us/me/you. Reflection, as stated in Chapter 1, is about skill and personal development. In order to develop as individuals, we have to get to know ourselves and then understand as much as we can about ourselves in every facet of life. However, this isn't an easy task.

The aim of this chapter to take a look at what we mean by attitudinal qualities and self-awareness. We will pay particular attention to how attitudinal qualities enhance our ability to reflect and help us to gain greater levels of self-awareness, and how having a level of self-awareness supports and enhances reflection. It is important to note that it is not the intention of this chapter to give you self-awareness, but to enable understanding of why this concept is important and to provide you with hints and tips of how to start gaining more self-awareness.

Let us first look at how our third and fourth essential ingredients – attitudinal qualities and self-awareness respectively – interact together.

## Essential ingredient #3 – *Attitudinal qualities*

*'The driving force of successful engagement with the reflective process. The practitioner needs to be humble to the process, be open, honest, and willing, having the motivation to understand and learn. The practitioner needs to be brave, courageous, and confident in order to encourage the honesty required in the process. Kindness, compassion, and offering unconditional positive regard to oneself enable openness.'*

(Adapted from Clarke 2014)

### Exercise 3.1: Attitudinal qualities

Read the description of our third essential ingredient above. In the space below, jot down why you think this is an important ingredient in supporting the reflective process.

The qualities described above are important because:

### Exercise 3.2: Self-awareness

Now write down how you would describe yourself to other people.

I would describe myself as:

We can all provide colourful descriptions of ourselves to another person – this is called our *self-perception*, or having a basic level of self-awareness. When thinking about this in relation to reflection, it is common for students also to know exactly how they felt during a particular experience. I often see and hear statements such as:

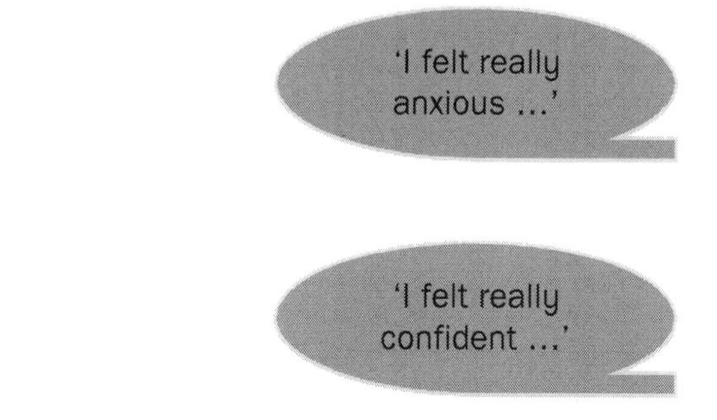


Or:

In Exercise 3.2, you jotted down words and statements that you perceive describe you. However, such words and statements are just a description of what you think and feel about yourself – just like the reflective statements about feelings in the speech bubbles above. What you did here was a simple act of *describing*. What is of real importance is whether you know *why* you described yourself the way you did in Exercise 3.2. This is a deeper level of self-awareness and a level that we have to want, and be open to gaining. The attitudinal qualities of humility, honesty, openness, willingness, bravery, courage, and confidence to change are key ingredients. These qualities are the scaffolding that supports the process of gaining a deeper understanding of what lies behind your self-perception descriptors, and which will ultimately enhance your self-awareness.

## What do we mean by attitudinal qualities?

Before we consider the different aspects of the ingredient attitudinal qualities, let us consider what we mean by *attitude*. Early writers offered quite broad definitions of *attitude* that encompassed cognitive (thoughts), affective (emotions), motivational (enthusiasm), and behavioural (action) components. For example, Allport, a prominent writer in the field of psychology, defined an attitude as:

> A mental and neural state of readiness, organized through experience, exerting a directive and dynamic influence upon

> the individual's response to all objects and situations with which it is related.
>
> (Allport 1935: 810)

Put simply, what Allport is suggesting here is that our attitude (the way we think and feel) directs our responses (the way we behave) to the experiences that come our way. Let's think about this in relation to the first part of the ingredient that is attitudinal qualities:

> 'The practitioner needs to be humble to the process, be open, honest, and willing, having the motivation to understand and learn.'

Breaking this first part down in relation to the reflective process, this ingredient is asking us, as the reflectors, to:

- be respectful of the process (we might just learn something!);
- recognize we could learn something (after all, do we really know everything about ourselves?);
- be enthusiastic about the potential for learning.

In other words, *be okay with not knowing everything and be okay with getting to know yourself in the reflective process!* If we take this on board, we will then behave in a manner in the reflective process that opens the way for learning.

Now let's take a look at the second part of the ingredient we call attitudinal qualities:

> 'The practitioner needs to be brave, courageous, and confident in order to encourage the honesty required in the process.'

Ask yourself, when you started to learn about reflection, did you realize that to reflect properly you would need to be brave and honest? I can imagine your answer to be, 'no, not really!' But reflect on the following experience:

*Scenario 3.1: An uncomfortable situation*

You are supporting your mentor to care for a patient who raises your anxiety. This patient has dementia. You are alone with this person and you don't know what to say to them when they think you are their daughter. You try very hard to convince them you are not – you think this is best for them. The patient becomes agitated and very upset. Your mentor comes to support you and helps the patient to settle.

You internalize the patient's reaction to you and believe you have done something wrong. You dwell on this and worry.

The easiest option here is to ignore your feelings and thoughts and simply to continue – not to learn from the experience but to shy away from it. However, this kind of experience can remain with us. It can inhibit our future engagement with our service users, our patients, and our carers. We can become fearful of re-experiencing such a situation. And when the same situation does indeed arise again, the negative feelings about ourselves taken from the new experience only add to those we already had from the first experience we did not learn from. We might eventually cease to enjoy being on placement or at work.

Although the above scenario cannot be considered too awful or unusual an experience, if we were not to learn from it, and then experienced further uncomfortable situations that we did not reflect upon, our minor fears could develop into something more serious.

So, we need to be brave. We need to have confidence in ourselves as people, and recognize ourselves to be kind, compassionate, and caring. We must realize we mean no harm, and that we are still learning. Thus we need to reflect. We need to be honest with ourselves about what we experienced, as well as honest about the feelings and thoughts we had at the time. We need to recognize we perhaps could have handled the situation a little better, but that that we cannot know everything. We should seek support from our mentor, evaluating the experience with them – using their wisdom and knowledge to increase our own. We need to read the evidence on caring for people with dementia and we need to learn from what happened. By doing so, we will develop both personally and professionally.

Now let's take a look at the third and final part of the ingredient that is attitudinal qualities:

'Kindness, compassion, and offering unconditional positive regard to oneself enable openness.'

The most important thing here is the reference to offering *unconditional positive regard to ourselves*. As nurses and healthcare practitioners in our person-centred practice, it is expected we will be non-judgemental towards the people we care for. But we don't always recognize the need to apply this expectation to ourselves. But what does this term mean? Carl Rogers, a prominent psychologist, one of the founders of Humanism – a theoretical paradigm – and the founder of the person-centred approach to counselling, likened unconditional positive regard to a feeling and generation of warmth and acceptance towards, along with a prizing of, the people we care for (Rogers 1957; Mearns and Thorne 1988; Bozarth 2002). We ultimately accept people for who they are, allowing them to have their own opinions, attitudes, morals, and values: we do not impose ourselves upon them, but neither do we have to agree with them. We offer them kindness and compassion. But what does this mean for us?

Have you ever said to yourself?

'I mustn't think like that.'

'I mustn't feel this way.'

What we are doing here is telling ourselves off and denying our right to think and feel a certain way for fear of being judged by others that we are different or wrong. When we do this to ourselves we become *incongruent*. We act in a different manner to how we think and feel. We brush our thoughts and feelings to one side and try to be something we are not, without first understanding our true selves. When we offer ourselves unconditional positive regard, we allow ourselves to accept our thoughts and feelings, we are kind to ourselves, and we don't tell ourselves off for thinking and feeling a certain way. We offer ourselves compassion through wanting to understand the nature of our thoughts and feelings. Once acceptance is allowed to occur, we can start to unpick/analyse why we think and feel the way we do. It is at this point we start to learn and gain insight into ourselves. Once understanding has occurred, we can begin to determine if change needs to take place. If we change, it is on the basis of understanding and choice, not ignorance and force. This type of change is then sustainable.

Take a look at the following two snapshots of two different students' reflective writing (we met these students in Chapter 2). Read carefully and then re-read the essential ingredient of attitudinal qualities.

*Scenario 3.2*

The female student who gave up wearing makeup for a week felt she had failed and relapsed by wearing lip balm.

> The second morning and I felt dreadful; I felt physically ill. I had plans made for today and needed to go out. Normally, when I'm ill I would still put on my makeup and face the day. Not today! I did look and feel awful and had conjunctivitis. This was going to be a trying day, as I was already having negative thoughts about how people would stare at me and I would feel very self-conscious. I had a pub breakfast with my husband and I was grateful not many people were in there. I chatted with the landlady but felt very conscious, particularly of my eyes. Before we set off where I would normally top up my lipstick I applied lip balm and a little extra moisturizer. Was I cheating? I told myself it wasn't, as my lips were dry due to my cold. On reflection I realized that this was a relapse and I was returning to my previous behaviours. It was only my second day. How was the rest of the week going to go if I am relapsing now? I did acknowledge the relapse and didn't see it as a failure. I had to learn to find a way to cope with the feelings of anxiety and self-awareness by keeping calm. I carried on with my planned day feeling very conscious, I hated catching a glimpse of my reflection in the mirror because I didn't recognize myself and didn't like what I saw.

*Scenario 3.3*

The male student who gave up tea and coffee for a week also felt he had failed before he had even started as he drank a cup of tea on his first day of abstaining:

Critical thoughts about my inability to control myself also started to arise. In turn, this generated negative emotional feelings that I would normally associate with low mood, in my body. At first, this failure seemed to me to be nothing more than a setback, a delay in my progress, a possible weakness in my character. However, when I thought about it some more, I started to think that there might be an important lesson to be learned from this initial 'failure' that might help me better understand substance misuse and abstinence. When I researched this I found that what I had been experiencing was 'ambivalence', which, according to a school of counselling called motivational interviewing, is understood to be a central obstacle to change [Miller and Rollnick, 2002] . . .

I now understand this lesson in the following terms: failure to abstain should not be understood as failure, but rather as an indicator of the presence of ambivalence in the mind of the abstainer, which may be rooted in a lack of preparation at the pre-contemplation stage. Understanding my 'failure' in these terms gave me plenty to work with and allowed me to feel hopeful about future attempts. For example, on reflection it seemed clear to me that I was not fully committed to abstaining from tea or coffee and that this was due to my lack of understanding and appreciation of the possibility that my tea and coffee consumption could be problematic and damaging. I clearly had some work to do in the pre-contemplation stage before I should attempt abstaining again

## Exercise 3.3: Who has the attitudinal qualities?

Now take a look at these snapshots in light of the ingredient that is attitudinal qualities:

- Can you see a difference between the two?
- What are those differences?
- Who has been honest?
- Who has been brave and courageous?
- Who has really opened themselves to learning?
- Who has offered themselves unconditional positive regard?
- Who has really tried to understand their thoughts and feelings?

You may see something of all these elements in both snapshots. But what you will see is that these elements are engaged with on different levels and only one of the students really tries to understand their experience.

What you need to do now is to consider how the ingredient of attitudinal qualities applies to you. So think about where you feel you are in relation to these qualities. Do you have these qualities and, if so, to what degree?

## Exercise 3.4: Your current positioning in relation to the attitudinal qualities

Jot down in the table below what you think and feel about each of the qualities. Note that as an aid, the columns for being 'open to learning' have been filled in for you.

***Positioning*:** Do you feel you have this quality and, if you do, to what degree?
***Experience*:** Reflect on and identity an experience you have had that would support your view. Have you had any experiences that could be used to question or disagree with your view?
***Learning*:** What do you feel you have learned about yourself undertaking this exercise and why?
***Development*:** Have you identified areas that require development?

**Table 3.1** My qualities

| Quality | Positioning | Experience | Learning | Development |
|---|---|---|---|---|
| **Open to learning** | Relatively open to learning new things. Perhaps more so in my role as student, but less so in my personal life | I ask questions of my mentors, I spend time reading and researching topics, I get anxious on placement as I know I don't know an awful lot. But people who know me outside of nursing would describe me as quite opinionated | When I am out of my comfort zone I am well aware of my lack of knowledge and this makes me want to learn. When I think I know things, I realize that I close myself off to listening to others | I need to be more open to listening to and learning from others outside of being a student nurse. I need to be confident enough to recognize I might not always be right |

| Quality | Positioning | Experience | Learning | Development |
|---|---|---|---|---|
| Honest | | | | |
| Motivated | | | | |
| Brave | | | | |
| Kind to myself | | | | |
| Non-judgemental towards myself | | | | |

What you have done here is to reflect on practice. You have considered your experiences, and to a degree you have evaluated yourself in relation to those experiences. As a result, some learning has occurred that you can put into play when you need to. The result is that you have become a reflective practitioner!

## What do we mean by self-awareness?

Before we take a look at how all of this relates to the ingredient of self-awareness, you first need to understand what the term self-awareness means. Eckroth-Bucher (2010: 297) defined self-awareness as:

> The cerebral exercise of introspection. This attribute reflects the cognitive exploration of own thoughts, feelings, beliefs, values, behaviours, and the feedback from others.

In other words, self-awareness is the thoughtful consideration of oneself. Not just self-indulgently thinking of oneself, however, but making a conscious effort to understand and know your own identity, beliefs, thoughts, traits, motivations, feelings, and behaviours and to recognize how these can impact on you and on those around you. Hofstadter (2007) associated self-awareness with consciousness. In developing this notion we can say self-awareness is about recognizing we are conscious, we exist, and in that recognition we know we can think about our thoughts and actions. Luft and Ingham, two prominent psychologists, devised the Johari Window (see Figure 3.1) as a way of illustrating the concept of self-awareness.

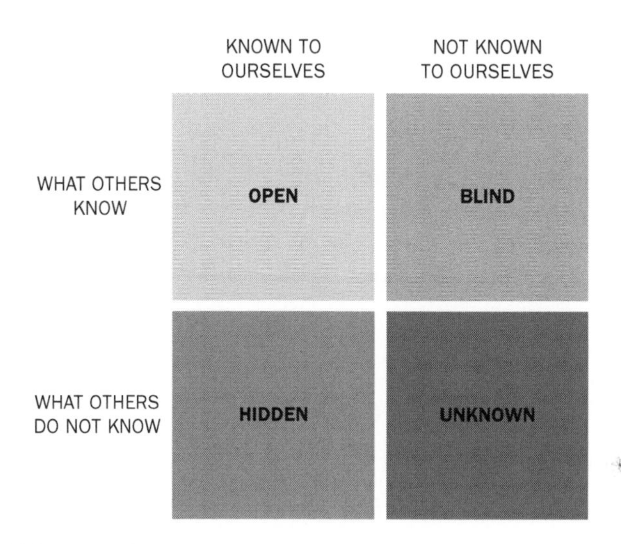


**Figure 3.1** Johari window

Source: Adapted from Luft and Ingham (1955).

The Johari Window has four quadrants:

1 The *Open* quadrant signifies what you know about yourself and is also known to those around you.
2 The *Blind* quadrant represents those things other people feel they know about you, that perhaps you do not know about yourself.
3 The *Hidden* quadrant recognizes there are things you know about yourself that others do not.
4 The final quadrant is classed as *Unknown*, things that neither yourself nor other people know about you.

Our aim in the reflective process is to make the *Open* quadrant the largest quadrant. The larger this is, the more self-awareness we have. That is not to say that you can't keep some things to yourself (*Hidden);* there may be some things about yourself that you may consciously choose not to tell others – this is okay. It is also important to note that the *Unknown* doesn't always have to remain unknown. You may have had an experience that tells you something quite surprising about yourself that neither you nor others were aware of. What is most important here is opening yourself up to getting to know your *Unknown* areas.

It also needs to be understood that our *Blind* area can diminish through the reflective process by encouraging feedback from others to support the expansion of our *Open* quadrant.

If you consider Exercise 3.4 in relation to the Johari Window, what you did was to tell us about your *Open* and maybe also aspects of your *Hidden* quadrant. So now let's see how much you understand these factors about yourself. Have a go at completing Exercise 3.5.

### Exercise 3.5: What is your level of self-awareness? Let's reflect on practice!

Take another look at Exercise 3.4 and ask yourself questions about each of the things you described yourself to be.

- Why would you describe this aspect as being part of who you are?
- What evidence do you have?
- What impact does this aspect have on you?
- What impact does this aspect have on those around you? What feedback have you received?
- How functional is this aspect of you? How well do you utilize this aspect of you? Does it work for you?
- What evidence do you have to support the functionality or non-funtionality of this aspect?
- Do you need to change?

To answer these questions in the best of your ability, you need to connect with the attitudinal qualities ingredient. So, to answer these questions to heighten your self-awareness, you need to be open, honest, brave, and non-judgemental of yourself. What you are doing here is connecting the ingredient of attitudinal qualities with the ingredient of self-awareness.

By looking at our fourth essential ingredient, self-awareness, we will see that we need a certain level of self-awareness to be able to reflect.

## Essential ingredient #4 – *Self-awareness*

*'The practitioner needs to have a current level of awareness of self, a perception of how they perceive themselves to be. It is this current knowledge of self that is the basis for the reflective process. Self-awareness allows the individual to be honest about how they perceive themselves to "be" in the experience. It is this existing knowledge of the self that is also agreed, challenged, developed, and overturned, in and by, the reflective process.'*

(Adapted from Clarke 2014)

Atkins and Murphy (1993) believe that self-awareness is the foundation skill upon which reflection and reflective practice are built. In essence, to be able to reflect, to *you need to know yourself* to some degree. It enables you to see yourself in a particular situation and honestly observe how you have affected that situation and how the situation has affected you. It further allows you to analyse your feelings regarding that particular event as the self-awareness you currently have ensures you already know what your thoughts and feelings are. Self-awareness is central to the ability to be self-critical, self-directing, and self-motivated (Smith 2011). If we look at this in relation to being a nursing student/healthcare practitioner, having a level of self-awareness when caring for vulnerable people allows you to recognize what your own value systems are and know that they may be different to the person you are caring for. It allows you to put these value systems to one side in order to understand the value systems of the person you are looking after.

To be able to learn from the reflective process, therefore, you need to be able to get to know yourself at a deeper level. However, developing this deeper level of honest self-awareness is not easy. Our current level of self-awareness may not be altogether fully unbiased. Atkins (2004) recognized that individuals have a tendency to want to portray themselves in a favourable light or in a positive frame – at the end of the day, who doesn't want people to see them as inherently good? However, it is this natural human tendency that can interfere with our ability to reflect objectively and ultimately gain that deeper understanding. In light of this, you will now see why the ingredient of attitudinal qualities –honesty, bravery, and so on – plays such a vital role not only in reflection and reflective practice, but in gaining the deeper levels of self-awareness that we need to be able to learn about ourselves and develop as practitioners and as people. It is having the attitudinal qualities required for the reflective process that helps remove our biased view of ourselves and opens us up to learning: 'It takes considerable time, effort, determination, courage and humour to initiate and maintain effective reflection' (Taylor 2006: 48).

Let's consider what we have learned so far. We know that our attitude plays a vital role in being able to reflect effectively and to take on board the learning that can occur from successful reflection. Some of the exercises in this chapter have been designed to enable you to begin to understand your own attitudinal qualities and highlight areas for your attitudinal development. We have learned that reflection generates self-awareness, but ironically we do need a level of self-awareness in order to reflect successfully in the first place! All of the exercises in this chapter will support you in generating greater levels of self-awareness.

Let's review what these exercises are asking us to do when getting to know ourselves. Have a go at completing Exercise 3.6.

We can determine from this exercise that all we are doing is asking lots of questions about the nature of our experiences and then trying to answer them. These questions are designed to probe quite deeply into our thoughts, feelings, and behaviours in the hope that the answers we give to ourselves will generate some knowledge that we can assimilate and use in the future. We are simply trying to get to know ourselves.

We can also undertake the same exercise in relation to the *Blind* quadrant of the Johari Window. Remember that the *Blind* quadrant

## Exercise 3.6: Generating self-awareness. Let us reflect on practice!

| The nature of the experience | Thoughts | Ask yourself |
|---|---|---|
| What happened?<br>What were you involved in?<br>Who was with you at the time? | Identify one thought you had that stands out for you | Why have I chosen this thought to reflect on?<br>What happened at the time to make me think this?<br>Why did I think this?<br>Did what happen justify my thought?<br>What values of mine do I believe made me think this way?<br>Was my thought influenced by anything else at the time – things, people?<br>What was the impact of that thought on my behaviour?<br>How did that thought make me feel at the time?<br>What impact did how I felt have on me at the time?<br>How did this affect me following the experience?<br>What do I feel I have learned about myself? |

is where others may know something about us that we do not. However, what others know can become known to us if we are open to learning – these aspects do not need to stay blind forever. A person we have come into contact with – a family member, mentor, friend, partner, boss – may choose to tell us something about ourselves we were unaware of. It could be how we come across to people in certain situations, how we make someone feel without realizing it, or it may be how we have responded to a patient. This does not always need to be a negative observation.

So now have a go at completing Exercise 3.7 and see if you can make something that sat in the *Blind* quadrant part of the *Open* quadrant.

## Exercise 3.7: Generating self-awareness. Let us acknowledge the *Blind* quadrant!

| The nature of the experience | Thoughts | Ask yourself |
|---|---|---|
| Recall an experience when someone told you something about you that you were unaware of:<br>What happened?<br>Who told you?<br>What were you involved in?<br>Who was with you at the time? | What was the person's observation, thought, feeling about you?<br>What did they tell you about yourself you did not know already? | Why have I chosen this to reflect on, what is the significance of this?<br>What happened at the time to make them highlight this to me?<br>What was my reaction to them on telling me?<br>What was I doing in order to make them see me in this light?<br>What values of mine do I believe made me behave this way?<br>Was my behaviour influenced by anything else at the time – things, people?<br>How do I feel about what they told me?<br>What was the impact of what they told me on my future behaviour, thoughts, feelings?<br>Do I agree with their observations about me?<br>What do I feel I have learned about myself? |

To recap, all we have been doing in the exercises in this chapter is to reflect on experiences. We have diligently considered our experiences, asking lots of questions and answering them.

It was the intention of this chapter to demonstrate how the two ingredients of attitudinal qualities and self-awareness play a vital role in the reflective process. We have shown how they support each other and if combined effectively allow us to gain deeper levels of understanding about the people we are and thus raise our levels of emotional intelligence. We can see how by engaging in the reflective process and combining these ingredients, we can develop as unique individuals with higher levels of self-awareness that will only help to support and enhance our clinical practice.

If we revisit the extended description of reflection, we can see where these two ingredients are situated:

> . . . understanding ourselves in relation to experiences we are about to have, are having or have had . . . then stepping beyond the self and using this knowledge gained to understand how we may then have impacted on those around us. For this process to be fruitful, we must leave arrogance and complacency at the door, be kind and compassionate, offering ourselves unconditional positive regard . . . open to learning . . .

**Key points that can be taken from this chapter are:**

- Attitudinal qualities play a vital role in ensuring effective, successful reflection occurs.
- Attitudinal qualities support our ability to become self-aware.
- A level of self-awareness is required to reflect.
- Reflection can generate much deeper levels of self-awareness.
- We need to be open to understanding ourselves.
- High self-awareness and the right attitude can engender good clinical practice.

CHAPTER

# Being person-centred and empathic

## Essential ingredient #5 – *Being person-centred*

*'The reflector has vast resources for self-understanding. These resources for self-understanding can be accessed if we are person-centred with ourselves. Recognizing we have our own unique subjective view of the world (our individual phenomenology) allows us to create a climate whereby we can get to know ourselves and gain a deeper understanding of ourselves in relation to our experiences. With understanding, a heightened level of self-awareness grows. We are able to develop both personally and professionally.'*

(Adapted from Clarke 2014)

## Essential ingredient #6 – *Being empathic*

*'The practitioner needs to want to understand themselves in relation to their experiences accurately. They need to use the skills of empathic questioning and responding to allow for deeper analysis of their thoughts, feelings, and behaviour in relation to what they are reflecting on. Not only this, they need to also be able to use their empathy to understand how others perceive them and the experience.'*

(Adapted from Clarke 2014)

## Learning outcomes

By the end of this chapter, you will be able to:

- Understand and appreciate the importance of being person-centred and how it supports successful reflection
- Determine how person-centred you are with yourself and be able to recognize areas for enhancement
- Understand the concept of empathy and the vital role it plays in reflective practice
- Use the knowledge gained to be person-centred and empathic with yourself in the reflective process.

In Chapter 3, we discussed the vital role that *attitudinal qualities* and *self-awareness* play in the reflective process. We acknowledged that in order to get to know ourselves at a deeper level in the process, we needed to have the attitudinal qualities (such as courage) needed for the learning about ourselves to take place, and so gain that greater level of self-understanding. The extended description of reflection asks us to take this a step further by using what we learned in Chapter 3 to become our own person-centred therapist, recognizing the need for us to accurately understand ourselves in the reflective process.

'The reflector has vast resources for self-understanding. These resources for self-understanding can be accessed if we are person-centred with ourselves.'

An integral part of being person-centred is the notion of empathy – embodying what it means to be empathic will support our endeavour to accurately understand ourselves within a person-centred framework:

> All nurses must act first and foremost to care for and safeguard the public. They must practise autonomously and be responsible and accountable for safe, compassionate, person-centred, evidence-based nursing that respects and maintains dignity and human rights.
>
> (NMC 2015b)

The Nursing and Midwifery Council (NMC) has recognized the importance of being person-centred by embedding the notion into their Code of Conduct (NMC 2015a) for nurses and midwives and their Standards for Competence for Registered Nurses (2015b). However, I believe the term person-centred – its relationship to care – is often used by students and qualified practitioners without fully understanding its meaning, its relevance to practice or to them.

## Two models of person-centred care

There are two models of person-centred care. The first, known as the *Eight Dimensions of Patient-Centred Care* (Figure 4.1), emerged from research conducted in the USA, with a key emphasis on recognizing each person as a unique individual holding different perspectives on life. The second model, the Person-Centred Nursing Framework (Figure 4.2), was developed by McCormack and McCance (2006, 2010) and comprises four constructs: the attributes of the nurse – *prerequisites*; the environmental context – *the care environment*; the processes that support being person-centred in care – *care processes*; and patient outcomes – *person-centred outcomes* (Tee and Newman 2016).

### Exercise 4.1: Is there anything missing?

Take a close look at Figures 4.1 and 4.2. Are there any aspects of a person-centred model of caring that you think are missing from either figure? Can you identify any differences?

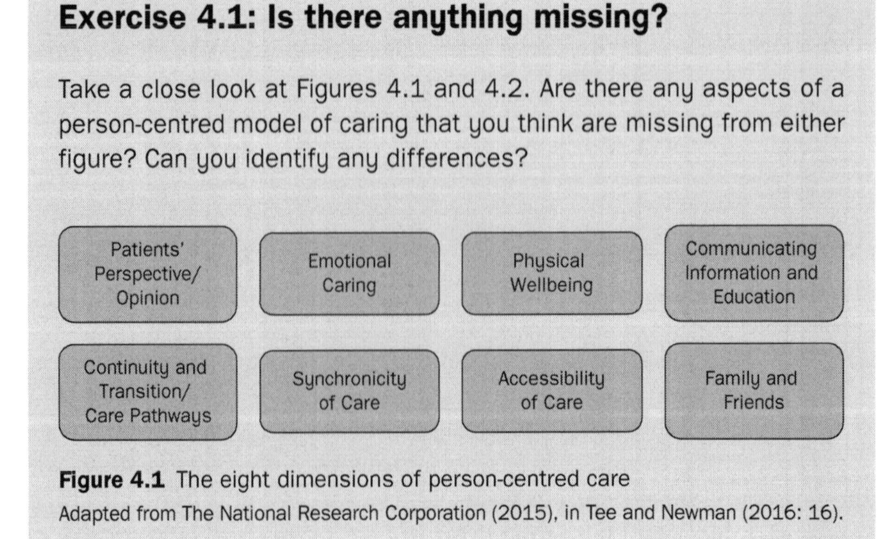


**Figure 4.1** The eight dimensions of person-centred care
Adapted from The National Research Corporation (2015), in Tee and Newman (2016: 16).

| Prerequisites of the nurse | The care environment | Care processes | Patient/person-centred outcomes |
|---|---|---|---|
| Professionally competent | Effective staff relationships | Working with patients' beliefs and values | Satisfaction with care |
| Has developed interpersonal skills | Supportive organizational systems | Engagement | Involvement with care |
| Committed to the job | Power sharing | Shared decision-making | Feeling of wellbeing |
| Clarity of beliefs and values | Potential for innovation and risk-taking | Having sympathetic presence | Creating a therapeutic culture |
| Knowing 'self' | Appropriate skills mix | Providing for physical needs | |
| | Shared decision-making systems | | |

**Figure 4.2** A person-centred nursing framework
Adapted from McCormack and McCance (2010), in Tee and Newman (2016: 17).

We can see that both models put the unique needs of the service user at the centre of their care, requiring that the helper view the service user holistically taking into account their own unique perspective. We can also see that both models rely on the therapeutic relationship and compassionate and sympathetic caring. However, one difference between the two is that the second model, the Person-Centred Nursing Framework, makes a clear reference to the attributes of the nurse – the prerequisites. If we look more closely at this figure we can see that *knowing 'self'* is a factor that McCormack and McCance (2006, 2010) believe nurses need to be person-centred in their care. It has already been acknowledged in detail that reflection allows us to get know ourselves, so in getting to know ourselves we will have the prerequisite to support person-centred practice that, according to McCormack and McCance (2006, 2010), is vitally important.

## What does it mean to be person-centred?

So, let's first look at our fifth essential ingredient – being person-centred.

## Essential ingredient #5 – *Being person-centred*

*'The reflector has vast resources for self-understanding. These resources for self-understanding can be accessed if we are person-centred with ourselves. Recognizing we have our own unique subjective view of the world (our individual phenomenology) allows us to create a climate whereby we can get to know ourselves and gain a deeper understanding of ourselves in relation to our experiences. With understanding, a heightened level of self-awareness grows. We are able to develop both personally and professionally.'*

(Adapted from Clarke 2014)

In this chapter, we are going to be taking a more in-depth look at the notion of being person-centred. We will not look in great detail at how it relates to care; instead, we will look at how it supports you in getting to know yourself and as a result enables and supports the reflective process. By really trying to understand what this notion means in relation to reflection, you will develop a better idea of what it means for care and clinical practice. We will take a close look at empathy. Empathy is a fundamental part of being person-centred, as we shall see in this chapter, and is a term that even seasoned practitioners sometimes misunderstand. Empathy is also in my opinion one of the most important concepts for us as practitioners to get our minds around. It underpins all types of therapeutic communication and ensures we understand our patients to a degree that supports person-centred practice.

### Exercise 4.2: Being person-centred

Consider your own understanding of the term 'being person-centred'. In the space below, jot down what this term means to you. We will come back to this at the end of the chapter to see if you come to view the notion differently once you have worked through the chapter.

I understand 'being person-centred' to mean:

The way in which I want you to understand the notion of being person-centred for the purposes of reflection requires me to introduce one of the most influential psychologists of all time, Carl Rogers (Kirschenbaum and Henderson 1989: xiii). Rogers, one of the founders of humanistic psychology and the founder of the person-centred approach to counselling, developed his own theory of personality and counselling. Unlike some counselling schools of thought, he believed that the counsellor should not simply adopt a set of tools and techniques for helping someone but adopt instead a *way of thinking and behaving* towards the individual requiring help.

Rogers believed that the helper has an attitude that consumes and, in simple terms, embodies the way they think, feel, and act towards another individual. It is these attitudinal qualities that provide the orientating framework within which the counsellor, helper or nurse views the world. Rogers referred to this attitude as a way of 'being' and was clear that the person-centred therapist, nurse or helper could be an imperfect person-centred practitioner as long as they did not perceive the approach as solely a set of techniques (Rogers 1951). Rogers was clear that in order to help another individual, one cannot make assumptions about what they are experiencing, thinking, and feeling; as a helper, we need to accurately understand that person we are helping and, in accurately understanding them, we can help them to understand themselves. The approach takes a non-directive stance, it doesn't look to solve people's problems for them, and it recognizes people as their own experts (Rogers 1951). Rogers believed that by embracing the person-centred approach, the practitioner could allow their personality to come through.

But what does this mean in relation to reflection and what does being person-centred mean when we apply it to ourselves in the reflective process?

Being person-centred with ourselves in the reflective process means that we wish to understand accurately how we think and feel about our own experiences. My own understanding of reality comes from understanding my subjective interpretation of the things I experience. Understanding the world and understanding me is about understanding what 'I' believe exists. We will not assume to know what we think and feel, or try and interpret why we think, feel, and behave the way we do. We are not going to tell ourselves how we should think and feel either. We just want to understand ourselves accurately. As a result, we shall get to know ourselves.

It is not my intention here to provide you with a theoretical lecture on Rogers' philosophy of therapy. Rather, the central assumption of Rogers' person-centred approach as it relates to reflection can be briefly stated as follows:

> It is that the individual has within himself or herself vast resources for self-understanding, for altering his or her self-concept, attitudes and self-directed behaviour – and that these resources can be tapped if only *a definable climate of facilitative psychological attitudes can be provided.*
>
> (Rogers 1986: 115–16/original emphasis)

Applying this quote to the reflective process, what we are interested in is the part that is in bold. In embodying what it is to be person-centred, we know that we have the ability to understand ourselves and from learning about ourselves we can fundamentally alter the way we then act in this world, although Rogers talks about this only happening if we provide the right climate for ourselves within which to grow and develop. It is this *climate* underpinning being person-centred, providing the framework for the reflective process, that we will look at more thoroughly in this chapter.

Consider this idea of providing a *climate.*

**Exercise 4.3: The climate for change**

In the space below, jot down what aspects/factors would need to be present when talking to another person in order for you to be open and honest about how you feel and think.

To be honest and open, there would need to be:

Rogers originally proposed that six conditions needed to exist for change to occur within a person. It is these six conditions that he suggested provide the climate for change. In the reflective process, for you to get to know yourself and allow change for the better to occur, you need to embody the six conditions shown in Table 4.1 and apply them (Rogers 1957).

**Table 4.1** The six necessary and sufficient conditions for therapeutic change

1. A client and a helper are in psychological contact
2. The client sees him or herself in need of help
3. The helper is congruent and genuine
4. The helper experiences unconditional positive regard towards the client in need of help
5. The therapist experiences an empathic understanding of the client's internal frame of reference and endeavours to communicate this experience to the client
6. The communication to the client of the therapist's empathic understanding and unconditional positive regard is to a minimal degree achieved.

Have a look at the conditions in the table. How does what you jotted down compare with the conditions in the table?

If you are at all familiar with Rogers' work, you may recognize the notion of the *three core conditions* (Figure 4.3). Over time, the six conditions for therapeutic change were simplified and combined – to become the three core conditions – by proponents of the person-centred philosophy. There are some who would criticize this simplification and suggest that this reduction has resulted in the misunderstanding that the therapeutic relationship within the person-centred framework is about 'doing to' rather than 'being with' the patient (Sanders 2006). But for our purposes of using this approach within the reflective process, the three core conditions provide a very useful climate within which we can safely get to know ourselves. So let's take a closer look at the three core conditions and see how they enable us to be person-centred with ourselves, creating the climate within which to reflect openly and honestly.

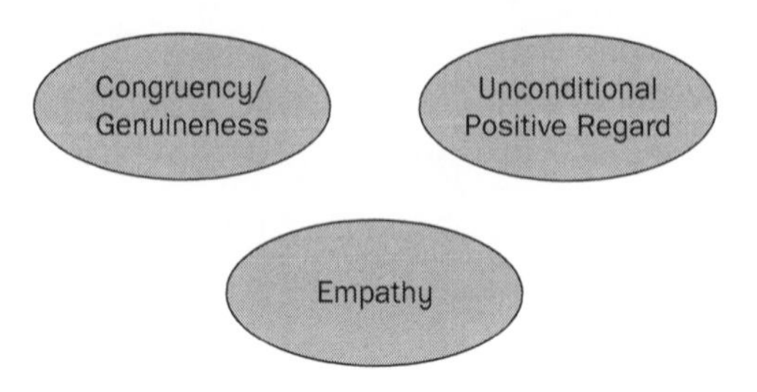


**Figure 4.3** The three core conditions

Since I view empathy as such an important condition, it is treated here as one of the Ten Essential Ingredients for Successful Reflection. Thus I will address empathy in the second part of this chapter. Let's first look at the other two core conditions in this model, the concepts of (1) genuineness/congruency and (2) unconditional positive regard.

## Genuineness and congruency

### Exercise 4.4: Exploring genuineness and congruency

In the space below, first jot down what you think 'being genuine and congruent' means. Then consider what this would mean in relation to you when reflecting. Finally, consider what it would mean when applied in the helping relationship with another person.

| *General meaning?* | *Meaning for you?* | *Meaning in relation to another?* |
|---|---|---|
| | | |

Let us consider this core condition in a little more detail before we review your own understanding in light of the new information.

Rogers proposed two meanings for this notion of being genuine and congruent. The first meaning relates to his patients coming to him for help in the counselling relationship. In this instance, being congruent means that our non-verbal and verbal behaviours towards another align with our genuine thoughts and feelings. So, for example, if you don't understand what the person you are caring for is trying to say, you shouldn't tell them that you do. Instead, you should verbalize that you are not clear as to what they mean and help them to explain in greater depth so you do eventually understand. The second relates to the person helping and their state of mind. We are also interested in the second meaning, as it relates to us in the helping relationship we have with ourselves when reflecting:

> The therapist should be, within the confines of this relationship, a congruent, genuine integrated person. It means that within the relationship the person is freely and deeply himself, with his actual experience accurately represented by his awareness of himself.
>
> (Rogers 1957: 97)

Let's simplify this. What this means for us in the relationship we have with ourselves in the reflective process is that we are open to ourselves. We are honest with ourselves about what we have experienced. We allow ourselves to be honest about how we think and feel about what we are experiencing and we don't try to be something we are not.

How many times have you said to yourself?

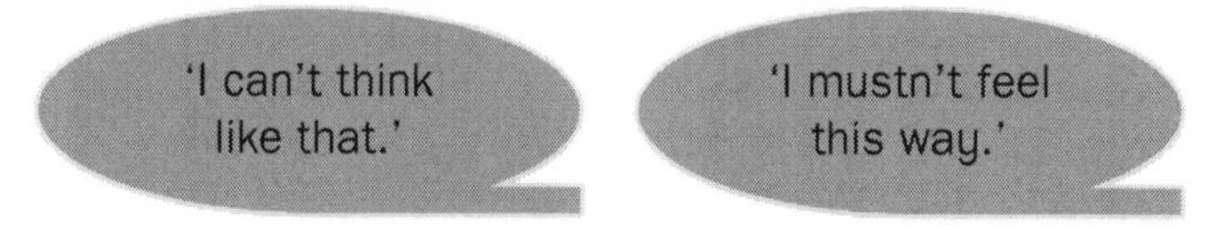


How helpful are we being to ourselves if we are not genuine and real about what we think and feel? The only way to understand ourselves is to be ourselves in the reflective process, not what we think others or society expects us to be. To understand this more clearly, let us briefly consider what this means in the helping relationship towards another person.

Take a look at Figure 4.4:

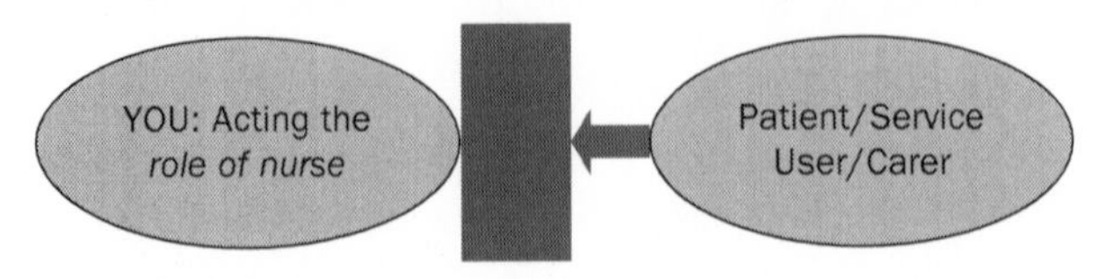


**Figure 4.4** Acting the role of nurse – lacking genuineness and congruency

When you act the *role* of the nurse, when you put up a professional façade, the person you are helping will try and connect with you, but won't be able to because the acting role will stop them from accessing you as a person. The rectangle in the figure represents the barrier that is created when you act the part, rather than allow your own personality to come through. As a helper, you should be confident enough in yourself that you allow yourself to be a real, authentic person with the individuals you are trying to help.

Let's consider this in relation to a person we are trying to help who perhaps is engaged in mental health services and whose own reality is perhaps far different from our own.

Service user:

'I see them, they are everywhere, and they are coming for me. Can't you see them too?'

The nurse who is confident enough in him or herself to be authentic and transparent might respond in the following way:

'No, I am sorry I cannot see what you are seeing right now. But I am trying to understand how what you are seeing is affecting you, you seem frightened?'

Here the nurse has been congruent. She has been respectfully honest with the service user; she has been real and authentic with compassion and kindness. The service user can connect with this nurse.

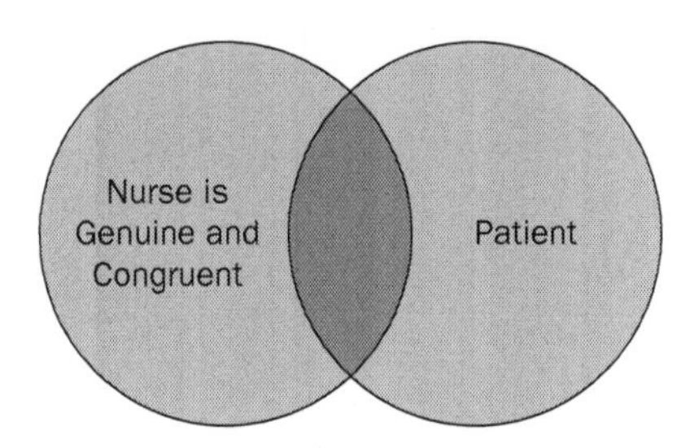


**Figure 4.5** When genuineness and congruency are present

As you can see from Figure 4.5, when the nurse embodies the notion of genuineness and congruency no barriers are present, the service user can connect, and the therapeutic relationship can now develop. The service user doesn't access the whole of the nurse, but the nurse's transparency allows the service user to view the nurse as a real person with thoughts and feelings of their own, not a cardboard cut-out of what they think a nurse should be.

So, let's relate this back to the reflective process. If when you are reflecting you are honest with yourself, congruent, and real about what you are or have thought and felt, you can access yourself and therefore gain a greater understanding of yourself. Take a look at Figure 4.6.

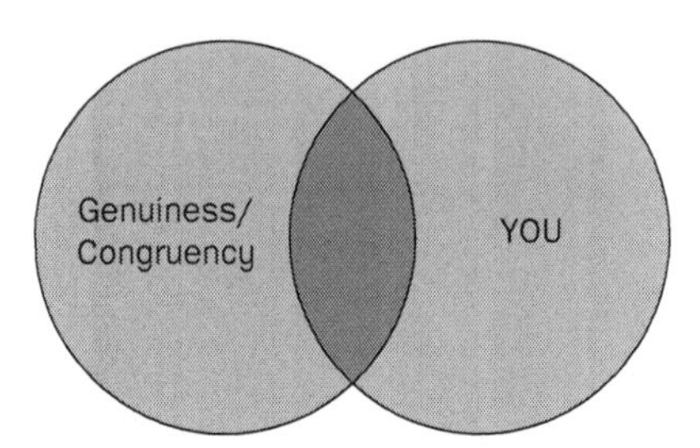


**Figure 4.6** Accessing yourself in the reflective process

Here, the two interconnecting circles represent the reflective process. The circles demonstrate how, by embodying the core condition of genuineness and congruency you are able to access and get to know yourself to the extent represented by the overlap of the circles.

Eventually, as you become more confident in being really honest with yourself, allowing yourself to be fully you when reflecting, there will only be a single circle, as you will be fully accessible to yourself. We can perhaps start to see now why what we discussed in Chapter 3 in relation to those attitudinal qualities is so important for this ingredient.

Now that we understand the core condition of *genuineness*, let's take a look at the core condition of *unconditional positive regard.*

## Unconditional positive regard

Unconditional positive regard has been a source of contention within the literature for a number of years – possibly prior to and certainly since Rogers in both his key papers stated: 'That the therapist is experiencing unconditional positive regards toward the client' (Rogers 1959: 213). Its importance, however, has been noted by the Nursing and Midwifery Council, which states that as nurses, 'You make sure that those receiving care are treated with respect, that their rights are upheld and that any discriminatory attitudes and behaviours towards those receiving care are challenged' (NMC 2015a).

Have a go now at the following exercise.

### Exercise 4.5: Defining unconditional positive regard

In the space below, jot down your understanding of unconditional positive regard.

I understand unconditional positive regard to mean:

Now consider your understanding of unconditional positive regard in relation to the following discussion before we contemplate how it is helpful in the reflective process.

Rogers perceived unconditional positive regard to be a warm acceptance of each aspect of the client's experience. Taking this into account, in order to offer unconditional positive regard, we need to recognize and accept every aspect of the person coming for help for who they are, with warmth and genuineness and without judging them. Furthermore, we need to recognize that they will need, eventually, to be able to understand themselves clearly, but before this can happen they need to accept themselves holistically. It is thought that offering unconditional positive regard supports acceptance on behalf of the person coming for help so that they can gain greater self-awareness (Dexter and Wash 2001).

It is the suspension of our own beliefs, ideas, and assumptions that underpins our ability to offer unconditional positive regard and, as a result, accept the person in need of help for who they are. In accepting the person in need of help for who they are, they will be able to begin to accept themselves.

However, it is important to note here that accepting the client for who they are and not judging them or offering an opinion does not mean that you agree with that person's beliefs, values or behaviour. When I discuss this notion of unconditional positive regard with my nursing students, the thought of acceptance and suspending one's personal judgements tends to create uncertainty and the impression that it also means agreeing with or condoning behaviour. However, this is not the case and, as already stated, *acceptance and being non-judgemental does not mean you are in agreement.*

Is this what you first considered unconditional positive regard to be? How does this compare with what you jotted down in Exercise 4.5?

Our next question is how does unconditional positive regard relate to the reflective process? As you will be aware from the previous chapters, reflection is about gaining greater self-awareness by getting to know ourselves in the reflective process. The offering of unconditional positive regard towards ourselves when we reflect, accepting ourselves for who we are, and not judging ourselves in relation to our thoughts and feelings allows us to feel accepted without being judged by the person most important to us – ourselves. As a result, we may feel free to be truly honest about our own thoughts and beliefs without fear of condemnation in the reflective process.

By not judging ourselves, we can be truly honest and as a result get to know and understand ourselves at a deeper level. Let's take another look at the aspects of the ingredient that is being person-centred. Can you see how unconditional positive regard connects to this ingredient?

> 'These resources for self-understanding can be accessed if we are person-centred with ourselves. Recognizing we have our own unique subjective view of the world (our individual phenomenology) allows us to create a climate whereby we can get to know ourselves and gain a deeper understanding of ourselves in relation to our experiences.'

And if we take another look at one aspect of the ingredient of attitudinal qualities from Chapter 3, we can see its relevance here too:

> 'Kindness, compassion, and offering unconditional positive regard to oneself enable openness.'

Take a look now at Scenario 4.1 and see unconditional positive regard in action.

*Scenario 4.1*

This female student is reflecting on her experiences of the caring process as a mental health nurse, looking after a pregnant drug user. She has allowed herself to be truly honest about what she thinks and how she feels. Ultimately, this will allow her to understand and accept herself, giving meaning to the learning taking place.

> My interactions also showed an element of co-dependency, I felt that if I was good enough, I could change her behaviour, not acknowledging that change has to come from within. I made decisions based upon what I thought Mary wanted me to do. I had created a dependent relationship, subconsciously perhaps to replace the dependency I had lost from my own daughter, and the dilemma now was if I discouraged this dependency would I be viewed as a loved mother, disapproving

but now rejecting mother, perpetuating her lifelong cycle of rejection and hopelessness.

I found my feelings regarding this transference and counter-transference to be very intense, agreeing with Ryum et al. (2010), who suggest that such reactions can provoke greater anxiety for both the client and professional, that transference and counter-transference can either impede the therapeutic relationship or provide an increased level of empathy.

## Being empathic

Let's now take a look at the sixth essential ingredient – being empathic.

### Essential ingredient #6 – *Being empathic*

*'The practitioner needs to want to understand themselves in relation to their experiences accurately. They need to use the skills of empathic questioning and responding to allow for deeper analysis of their thoughts, feelings, and behaviour in relation to what they are reflecting on. Not only this, they need to also be able to use their empathy to understand how others perceive them and the experience.'*

(Adapted from Clarke 2014)

Empathy is one of the most important ingredients to support understanding not only of yourself in the reflective process, but also understanding your service users in the person-centred caring process. The good news here is that empathy is strengthened by the first two core conditions of genuineness and unconditional positive regard that we have already discussed in relation to the fifth essential ingredient – that of being person-centred. Without these two conditions being in place, we cannot truly be empathic. As such, the first thing we need to acknowledge is that in being empathic we combine and embody the two components of attitude and skill. It is my belief that in being truly empathic, we cannot have one without the other.

To be truly empathic we need to embody the attitude of empathy, which is 'I am a transparent, accessible person with a genuine interest in the person I am caring for', or as in the case of reflection, a genuine interest in wanting to really get to know oneself. In other words, this attitude is an amalgamation of the first two core conditions in the person-centred framework. The second thing to consider is that empathy is also a skill set. The skills of empathic responding, which will be addressed in full in Chapter 5, combined with the right attitude, will enable the empathic process to be useful and to be experienced positively by the person you are caring for or by yourself when reflecting.

So, before we go any further and acknowledge some of the skills of empathic responding, we do need to consider carefully what we mean by being empathic. Have a go at the following exercise.

### Exercise 4.6: Defining empathy

In the space below, jot down your definition of empathy.

I would define empathy as follows:

When I ask my students what they think empathy is, they often respond as follows:

'Trying to view and see the world through someone else's eyes, then imagining what it would be like if it was.'

'Trying to imagine what someone is going through.'

Now bear these quotes in mind as we learn a little bit more about empathy and whether my students had an accurate understanding of this concept.

Empathy has been widely discussed in the literature for many years and a number of authors would acknowledge empathy has having three levels. The first level is often classed as *affective empathy* or *emotional contagion.* This is where, for instance, you are in a room full of students who are laughing and you can't help but laugh along with them. This level of empathy is the most basic and requires no understanding on your behalf as to why the group are laughing.

The next level of empathy has become a concept all on its own. This second level is when we experience concern, sorrow or sadness for another person (Wispé 1986); we don't understand their feelings and thoughts, yet we assume to know how the person is experiencing their reality. This has been termed *sympathy* and being a separate entity to that of empathy, it needs to be understood differently.

The final and most complex level of empathy is that with which we are most interested – the level of empathy when cognition (thinking) comes into play. Here, there is an appreciation of the feelings experienced by another, and an understanding of the other's internal world. This understanding is then communicated back to the other person (Rogers 1967) who perceives this empathy and uses it as a way of gaining greater self-understanding (Nelson-Jones 2006). Rogers suggested that in being empathic, you experience these feelings as if they are your own. But you never lose the 'as if' quality and never lose a sense of self. Empathy is a dynamic affective (emotional) and cognitive (thoughtful) complex process. Our aim as nurses and helpers when being empathic is to accurately understand how another person is experiencing their world without making assumptions. Being self-aware as we have previously discussed assists us in suspending our own assumptions and judgements so that we can really try to understand another from their own internal frame of reference (Rogers 1967; Brammer and MacDonald 1996). The communication skills discussed in the next chapter will support and enable you to be empathic.

Take a look at Exercise 4.7.

## Exercise 4.7: Empathy vs. sympathy

A female patient relates how she feels about her mum dying, but her feeling awful is not related to what one might assume results in this way of responding. She is left with feelings of confusion, that she has lost her sense of purpose, and she has no focus now that she has no one to care for having been her mum's full-time carer. She is happy for her mum that she is no longer in pain, yet feels sadness as she misses her mum and would like her to be alive and well. She also feels alone and yet guilty because she is now free to make other friendships.

Take a look at this first possible interaction between patient and nurse:

Patient: 'I feel awful since my mum passed away, nothing is the same and I feel guilty.'

Nurse: 'Oh I am so sorry to hear this, I know how you feel, and I felt exactly the same when my mum passed away.'

Now have a go at answering the following questions:

- What do you think the nurse is feeling towards the patient?
- Why do you think the nurse has responded in this manner? Which of the six necessary and sufficient conditions for therapeutic change do you think the nurse is demonstrating (see Table 4.1)?
- What type of a response is this – empathic or sympathetic?
- How do you imagine the patient is likely to respond?
- What do you think might be achieved?
- Do you think the nurse's response will enable the patient to give the nurse all the information as detailed above?
- In what other way might the nurse have responded?

Now take a look at a second possible interaction between patient and nurse:

Patient: 'I feel awful since my mum passed away, nothing is the same and I feel guilty.'

Nurse: 'I am sorry to hear about your mum passing, you say you feel awful since your mum passed away and things feel very different to you now. Is this something you would like to talk with me about?'

Now revisit the same questions above. Once you have answered the questions a second time, which would you consider to be the empathic response, whereby the nurse is trying to convey to the patient that she has heard and understood the patient's frame of reference, and that will encourage the patient to talk freely and openly?

Hopefully, you will have identified the second response as the empathic response. The first response, which is a sympathetic response, may convey a level of compassion to the patient but almost immediately it tells her that the nurse doesn't understand her, and may even inhibit the patient from talking to the nurse openly. Now what has this got to do with reflection?

In order to reflect properly and gain the most from the process, we need to be able to understand ourselves, but that understanding needs to be accurate – understanding that is based upon not assuming to know how we think and feel about things. Such an understanding needs to come from an exploration of our true thoughts and feelings. Take a look at the example of reflection-on-action in Box 4.1. Here you will see an example of reflection where empathy is not available to the reflector and an example of where the person reflecting has embodied the notion of reflection and used empathic responding skills to get to know themselves with accuracy.

## Box 4.1: Empathy in the reflective process – reflection-on-action

| *Without empathy* | *The experience* | *With empathy* |
|---|---|---|
| I don't know why I didn't really listen to her.<br>I think I just felt that having done some reading I knew best.<br>I have learned that I need to listen more and demonstrate I have heard the person more clearly. | I was supporting a lady in the community who was terrified of having a natural birth and was determined to move forward with a caesarean section. The lady was engaged with mental health services due to low mood, anxiety, and post-natal depression following the birth of her first child. She had also had a very traumatic natural birth with her first child where mum and baby both nearly died.<br>I strongly advised her to have a natural birth, advising that recovery from a caesarean section is prolonged and there can be complications. I did not support or listen to her when she was expressing her concerns about the natural birth; in fact, I was quite dismissive. As a result, I feel that I am now struggling to connect with her. | I didn't listen to her concerns with care and compassion. I have asked myself why. At first I believed it to be because I had done some reading around birthing methods and I felt I was being truly evidenced-based in my reaction. However, I have considered this more deeply and I recognize that I was bringing elements of myself into my interaction and it was clouding my judgement. Thinking about my own experiences of a caesarean section, I now recognize they were hindering my ability to truly hear her concerns. I have recognized here that my own experiences and feelings and thoughts about those experiences were not put to one side. This hindered my ability to be with this lady. |

Before we revisit the extended description of reflection, take another look at the exercises in this chapter where you have provided your own understanding of the concepts we have discussed. Would you now change those definitions in light of what has been discussed?

By revisiting the extended description of reflection here, we can see where the ingredients of being person-centred and being empathic are situated:

> Reflection is an essential, engaging process that allows the reflector to frame and reframe their reality that is being experienced moment by moment. It requires us to utilize skills of communication, to become our own person-centred therapists, understanding ourselves in relation to experiences we are about to have, are having or have had, empathically and with accuracy.

**Key points that can be taken from this chapter are:**

- Being person-centred plays a vital role in ensuring effective successful reflection.
- Being person-centred allows us to get to know our true selves.
- The core conditions of genuineness, unconditional positive regard, and empathy are the corner-stones of being person-centred.
- You cannot truly be empathic without embodying the core conditions of genuineness and unconditional positive regard.
- In order to truly understand yourself, you have to assume not to know – and you need to want to get to know – yourself with accuracy.
- Empathy enables the accuracy of the reflective process.
- Being person-centred is a way of 'being'.

CHAPTER

# Communication and mindfulness

**Essential ingredient #7 – *Communication***

*'The practitioner needs to be able to articulate themselves in a verbal and non-verbal manner, whether this is to themselves or to another person. They need to have the communication skills that allow them to act as their own internal supervisor. These communication skills include the skills of Socratic questioning and empathic responding.'*

(Adapted from Clarke 2014)

**Essential ingredient #8 – *Mindfulness***

*'The practitioner needs to be cognisant of themselves, their surroundings, their behaviour, thoughts, and feelings. An acute awareness of the experience they are having or have had moment by moment and in the context of others.'*

(Adapted from Clarke 2014)

## Learning outcomes

By the end of this chapter, you will be able to:

- Demonstrate an understanding of communication and how it supports successful reflection
- Understand the terms Socratic dialogue and empathic responding
- Articulate the meaning of 'internal supervisor'
- Use the basic skills of Socratic dialogue and empathic responding in the reflective process, whether with another person or when acting as your own internal supervisor
- Demonstrate knowledge of the term mindfulness
- Know how mindfulness is connected to the reflective process.

In the previous chapter, we addressed the important role *person-centredness* and *empathy* play in the reflective process. We took a detailed look at these terms and their relationship with reflection. We discovered that being person-centred with ourselves when reflecting allows for a deeper understanding of our true selves. It allows us to be free and honest with our thoughts and feelings. We also established that the third core condition of the person-centred approach – empathy – is fundamental to empowering and enabling us to be person-centred. However, we also saw that empathy is not only a case of truly wanting to get to know ourselves from our own unique perspective but also a set of communication skills. If we take a look at the following element of the extended description of reflection, we can see reference to a further dimension of person-centeredness:

> 'It requires us to utilize skills of communication, to become our own person-centred therapists, understanding ourselves in relation to experiences we are about to have, are having or have had, empathically and with accuracy, then stepping beyond the self and using this knowledge gained to understand how we may then have impacted on those around us.'

This further dimension asks us to use the knowledge gained about ourselves in the reflective process from being person-centred and consider what we have learned in the context of others. This means we need to be reflexive and mindful.

The aims of this chapter are twofold: first, to explore communication as it relates to the reflective process, in particular identifying the skills of Socratic dialogue and empathic responding and how we can apply these skills to ourselves when reflecting; and second, to discuss mindfulness in the context of the reflective process and how it also relates to the notion of reflexivity.

## Communication skills

Let's first take a look at our seventh essential ingredient – communication skills.

### Essential ingredient #7 – *Communication*

*'The practitioner needs to be able to articulate themselves in a verbal and non-verbal manner, whether this is to themselves or to another person. They need to have the communication skills that allow them to act as their own internal supervisor. These communication skills include the skills of Socratic questioning and empathic responding.'*

(Adapted from Clarke 2014)

Have a go at completing Exercises 5.1 and 5.2.

### Exercise 5.1: Exploring your knowledge of communication

Having read the previous chapters and drawing on your experience from your training to date, jot down in the space below why you think communication is vital in the reflective process.

Communication is vital to the reflective process because:

### Exercise 5.2: Communication skills

Again drawing on what you already know about communication in the caring professions, jot down what communication skills you think are required in order to reflect fully.

I believe the following communication skills are required to reflect fully:

We all communicate to some degree or another. We know we communicate in different ways. The fact that we are referring here to communication skills implies that ways, methods, and techniques of communicating are, over time, practised, developed, and hopefully used with a purpose in mind. In nursing, communication skills such as listening and the use of both verbal and non-verbal cues are integral to the development of the therapeutic relationship with the person you are caring for. Listening in nursing not only allows you to gather accurate information, but if you listen actively – that is, concentrating on what the person is telling you, really trying to hear what they are saying, and relaying back to them that you understand – it allows the service user to feel heard and understood, which ultimately enables them to open up to you more. This process of actively listening is aided by your verbal and non-verbal skills. In the therapeutic relationship, the use of these verbal and non-verbal skills and engagement with patients and other members of staff on hospital wards and other areas in which you work will develop over time. What we wish to do here is develop these skills in relation to *yourself* in the reflective process.

This is not a simple task, as it is not every day you are asked to consider how you communicate with yourself. So before we move forward, ask yourself how often you talk to yourself. How often do you actually stop and have a conversation with yourself about what you are experiencing? I would suggest possibly not as often as you will do once you have finished reading this book and become proficient at being your own *internal supervisor.*

## The internal supervisor

In Chapter 1, we acknowledged the different times when reflection can occur. You may remember that we can reflect both 'on' and 'in' action (see Figure 5.1). In the literature, it is acknowledged that spontaneous reflection in-action is not only a product of the development of reflecting on-action skills but of the development of our internal supervisor (Casement 1985; Bond and Holland 1998; Todd 2005). Let's consider what we mean by the idea of the internal supervisor.

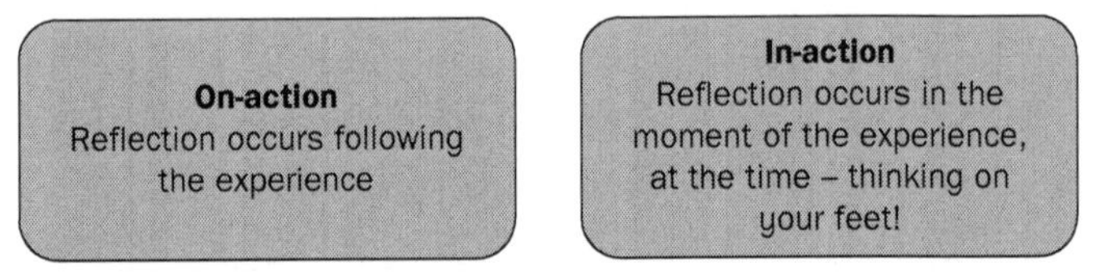


**Figure 5.1** Reflection-on-action and reflection-in-action

The notion of the 'internal supervisor' was devised as a metaphor to describe the dialogue that occurs in our minds when we reflect within the moment of the experience (Todd 2005), or the conversation that a person holds with him or herself internally about an event as that event is unfolding. The internal supervisor (you) will question personal bias (judgements) and subjectivity in the hope that you will enable yourself to find a more objective perspective and way of looking at something (Todd 2002). The internal supervisor is a way of questioning the self or yourself at the time of engaging in any given situation – it allows you to be fully aware of your own engagement and to be mindful of the potential outcome.

The internal supervisor will listen more than it will talk but it will use skills of communication that include Socratic dialogue and empathic responding, which we will address later in this chapter. By activating our internal supervisor, we are able to reflect in-action, or become mindful. For example:

'I felt really insecure about what I was doing. I think my mentor was waiting for me to fail, she was watching me over my shoulder ...'

'Waiting for me to fail? Do I really think this person wanted me to fail, what did she do that would make me think that?'

This does, however, take practice and Johns (2000) has acknowledged that there are limits to reflecting alone, and that guided reflection with another person who can take over the role of internal supervisor can allow the reflective process to become more meaningful. However, if we have no one to reflect with and we want to reflect in the moment or after the moment, we need to understand the types of communication skills needed by our internal supervisor. These skills relate to the two terms we have previously acknowledged: Socratic dialogue and empathic responding.

## What is Socratic dialogue?

Socratic dialogue refers to systems devised by the Greek philosopher Socrates termed 'Socratic methods'. In simple terms, Socratic dialogue aims to question our preconceived ideas and pre-determined knowledge. It assumes 'not to know' and, through asking probing questions that require evidence for an answer, aims to achieve a deeper level of understanding about a very particular topic. The aim of Socratic questioning and dialogue is to explore through 'guided discovery' the content and meaning of experiences to enable learning to take place, and thus allow for change to occur in cognition/thought and behaviour (Wells 1997). When applied to ourselves, this type of dialogue is a communication method that allows for a deep analysis of self, through probing and gentle questioning – for which there may be no answers – enabling us to become more deeply familiar with our own selves (Ciarrochi and Bailey 2008).

Have a go at Exercise 5.3.

I'm guessing that that wasn't the easiest of tasks for you. But as I stated earlier, the more you practise the easier it will become.

## Exercise 5.3: Types of questions for a Socratic dialogue

Have a look at the scenario below. This scenario is about you recalling an experience you have had. Your recall may be based on having written this experience down as in the example below, or you may have simply remembered it and be left with feelings that arose as part of the experience, or that arose following the experience. In the column to the right, jot down questions that you would ask yourself that would allow you to provide more information. Record your responses to give you a greater understanding of what you went through. Remember what you are trying to do here is probe more deeply and gain a greater understanding of the experience. Remember, we don't want to make assumptions about ourselves. Instead, by being person-centred and using Socratic dialogue, we want ourselves to explore the things we say we feel, and think more deeply, to question, dispute or confirm our thoughts and feelings.

| ***Recalling the experience*** | ***Your questions and responses*** |
|---|---|
| That was my first assessment. I know it didn't go well. I think my mentor is disappointed in my performance. I upset the patient. They didn't respond to me well at all. I feel awful. I am not sure I want to go back on placement tomorrow. What if my mentor asks me to do another assessment and I am just as rubbish? | |

Now let's take a look at a model of reflection that will provide a framework for you until you are proficient and comfortable holding a Socratic dialogue with yourself.

Reflective models will be discussed in more detail later in the book when we review some of the most common cycles and models. But for now let us focus on Box 5.1. As we can see, Johns' model of structured reflection is composed of a series of questions that should help you when reflecting to focus in on a specific experience, and by using the questions highlighted in bold to hold a more Socratic dialogue with yourself. This model of reflection is likely more useful if you are reflecting alone and are a novice reflector requiring a more

## Box 5.1: A model of structured reflection

**Reflective cue:**

- Bring the mind home – re-immerse yourself in the experience
- **Focus on a description of an experience that seems significant in some way**
- **What resonated with me most starkly, what particular issues seem significant enough to demand attention?**
- **How do I think others were feeling, and what do I think made them feel that way?**
- **How was I feeling and what made me feel that way?**
- **What was I trying to achieve, and how did I respond?**
- *What were the consequences of my actions on the patient, others, and myself?*
- **What factors influenced the way I was feeling, thinking or responding?**
- What knowledge informed or might have informed me?
- **To what extent did I act for the best and in tune with my own values?**
- **How does this situation connect with previous experiences?**
- How might I respond more effectively if the same circumstances were to arise again?
- *What would be the consequences of alternative actions for the patient, others, and myself?*
- **How do I NOW feel about this experience?**
- Am I more able to support myself and others as a consequence?
- Am I more able to realize desirable practice monitored using appropriate frameworks such as framing perspectives, Carper's fundamental ways of knowing, and other maps?

Source: Adapted from Johns (2004: 3).

structured format. Johns' model is aimed at helping us to gain an empathic understanding of self, in relation to the experience we have had. This model does not assume that we know the questions to ask of ourselves. It does, however, require us to act in a non-judgemental way and offer unconditional positive regard towards ourselves while reflecting, otherwise the honesty that forms part of the basis for any effective reflection may be hindered or reduced.

This model also asks us to consider ourselves in the context of others, and asks the reflector to take into account the impact they may have had on those around them while in their own experience. The questions in italics require us to be reflexive and mindful, which again will be discussed later in the chapter. However, what it doesn't do is to give us the extra probing responses and questions to really understand ourselves accurately and allow us to feel heard. These are the skills of empathic responding.

This type of reflective conversation that we have with ourselves, engaging our internal supervisor in a conversation that includes the skills of Socratic dialogue and empathic responding, is of utmost importance. It is an interactive process that allows us to construct and re-construct meaning and action related to our experiences, called *framing and reframing* by Schön (1983). If we perceive something we have experienced to be really awful and we believe ourselves to be totally at fault, framing and reframing will allow us to reflect using Socratic dialogue and empathic responding techniques to view our experience quite differently. Indeed, by reframing the experience, we might conclude we were not at fault. So instead of ruminating and internalizing an incorrect interpretation of our experiences, the reflective process can help us to internalize the experience more positively. At the least, it will enable us to learn something about ourselves.

Let's now take a look at what we mean by empathic responding skills. Rogers was very clear when he suggested that true empathy is free of any judgement or analytical quality (Rogers 1980). Thus our responding skills need to be skills that probe our inner world and allow us to express accurately what we truly think and feel about our experiences.

Have a go at completing Exercise 5.4.

Now compare what you wrote down with the following:

- open questions;
- reflecting – parrot phrasing – mirroring;
- paraphrasing;
- exploring;
- clarifying;
- understanding ambivalence.

## Exercise 5.4: Empathic responding skills

In the space below, jot down ways of responding to a person or yourself in an empathic manner. What types of communication skills do you know that would allow you to tell yourself in more detail what you think and feel, and also allow you to check the accuracy of your understanding?

What empathic responding skills might I use?

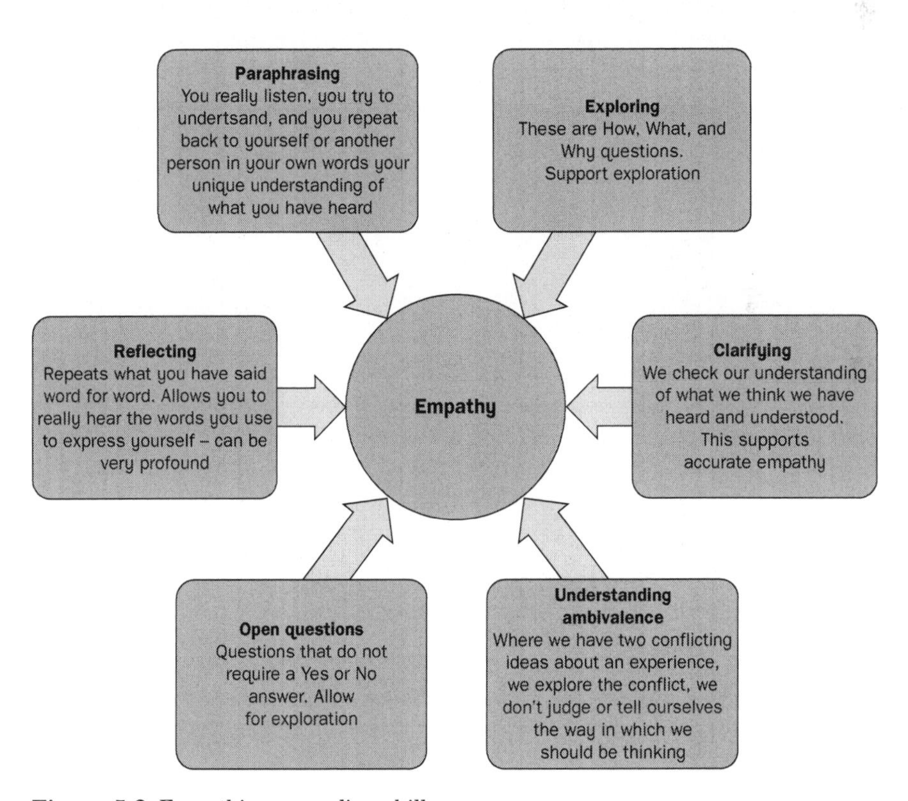


**Figure 5.2** Empathic responding skills

Did you record any of these empathic responding skills? None of these skills involves making interpretations, analysis or guesswork. They are all underpinned by the discussion on being person-centred we had in the previous chapter. Figure 5.3 details what each of the communication skills of empathic responding entails.

A word or two is required about ambivalence. This is a term that is part of a counselling school of thought called 'motivational interviewing'. Having used motivational interviewing a lot with my service users who have a substance misuse disorder, I find it to be extremely useful in the person-centred helping relationship and as such you can apply it to yourself in the reflective process. Ambivalence is a common state that occurs when contradictory or incompatible emotions or attitudes co-exist in the same individual, and tension arises as a consequence (Miller and Rollnick 2002). Asking questions about the ambivalence in order to understand it in the reflective process can also help you to resolve your ambivalence. Here are a couple of examples of incompatible thoughts.

'I really want to stop using heroin, I hate my life, but I can't as it's the only thing that keeps me feeling normal ...'

'I really want help with my numeracy exam but I don't want to ask as I feel stupid doing so ...'

Here we can see two different types of ambivalence. The first is typical ambivalence often displayed by my service users with substance misuse issues. The second is not untypical of my students who are concerned about what people will think of them if they ask for help. When asking ourselves questions, we may uncover ambivalence in some conflicting ideas or thoughts that arise.

Before we look at our next essential ingredient, mindfulness, practise these skills on yourself when reflecting. Practise on your friends, family, and work colleagues; try and use them in general conversation. This way, it will eventually become natural for you to embody what it means to be empathic and using it yourself when reflecting will become easier.

## Mindfulness

Now let us take a look at our eighth essential ingredient – mindfulness.

### Essential ingredient #8 – *Mindfulness*

*'The practitioner needs to be cognisant of themselves, their surroundings, their behaviour, thoughts, and feelings. An acute awareness of the experience they are having or have had moment by moment and in the context of others.'*

(Adapted from Clarke 2014)

It was acknowledged earlier in this chapter that the extended description of reflection asks us to use the knowledge gained about ourselves from being person-centred in the reflective process and to consider what we have learned in the context of others. Now that we also have the communication skills we need to get to know ourselves accurately, we can take this a step further and become *reflexive and mindful*. Mindfulness means being aware of oneself both moment to moment but also in the context of others. So let us consider what being mindful means and how it can relate to being reflexive.

Have a look at the following experience, which is based on the memory of giving my first injection.

I remember being in the second year of my four-year degree in mental health nursing. I had been given an adult branch placement in the hospital general setting. My mentor was supervising me give my very first injection. This, I recall, was a heparin injection. In my mind's eye, I can remember the needle being and feeling huge with a great big scoop on the end. I remember the older patient's tummy being very wrinkly and leathery. I remember watching almost in slow motion as my hand darted the needle towards the skin and then it bounced off! I remember my heart being in my mouth, sweating, shaking, and so hoping that my mentor would take over from me, which she did not do. She made me do it again. The second time I managed to complete the procedure successfully. I recall an immediate sense of relief, feeling very proud of my young self, and hoping never to give another injection again!

Back then, when I was 19 years old, I remember my reflections focused mostly on me rather than anything else. I reflected diligently on how I felt, and why I felt the way I did, I reflected conscientiously on how I could have done things better and what I had learned from the experience. But now when I look back and remember, not once did I consider how my experience might have affected the person I was caring for. Not once did I consider how he might have experienced me. I did reflect on how I felt about hurting him, but I did not reflect on how my nervousness and anxiety around hurting him impacted upon him. I did not consider how my thoughts, feelings, and behaviour might have affected my mentor who was attempting to teach me. So, although as a novice reflector I reflected quite well and I did learn things about me, it was in isolation from others and, it was to a degree, self-indulgent rumination. So being mindful helps to prevent what Bolton (2010) termed self-indulgent rumination.

What is meant by mindfulness in the context of reflection? According to one prominent writer in the field of reflection and nursing, reflective, mindful practice is framed as a 'way of being: a way that honours the intuitive and holistic nature of experience' (Johns 2005: 7). Note how this is not too dissimilar to the notion of being person-centred and embodying this notion as a *way of being*. Viewing reflection as being in a relationship and connected with the notion of mindfulness allows us to understand reflection as something that can be spontaneous, in the moment, at the time. It allows us to personify the notion of reflection and to reflect moment-by-moment, not just 'in' or 'on' practice. Johns (2005) further suggests that mindfulness is not only the thoughtful exclusion of everything except that which is being attended to, when attached to reflection it provides a framework within which we can view ourselves as a moment unfolds. But when being mindful, we don't just sit back and watch things happening to us. It is not a passive process. Instead, mindfulness in the reflective process means we are truly engaged with the unfolding situation, and embody all aspects of reflection so that we are able to understand ourselves at the time.

Bolton (2010) suggests mindfulness means that you are fully conscious of your actions, which in turn enables awareness of the likely outcome and appropriateness of the actions to be taken. Let's take, for example, reflection before action. When adopting mindfulness, you don't just blunder into a situation unprepared, but contemplate, cogitate, and reflect upon the situation about to be encountered – though this could simply be classed as conscientious nursing practice. As a student or as a qualified practitioner, before you embark on a new course of action (maybe you are giving a medication you have not given before, or meeting a new patient), you should always diligently think about and evaluate what you are about to do. You may know that you do this, so all we are doing here is giving a name to something you already ensures happens.

Mindfulness is a way of moving to a more purposeful way of perceiving experiences from a range of viewpoints and potential scenarios. Bolton (2010) likens the mindfulness in reflection to a game of chess in which a player (the reflector) does not make a move without considering first its impact on the rest of their own and their opponent's pieces, and what it might mean for the game as a whole (the experience). Thus, the player considers moving the piece not in isolation, but in among all the other chess pieces (life, work, and people) and how their next move will impact upon the outcome of the game. This leads us effectively to the notion of reflexivity.

Reflexivity as an independent notion has been discussed and analysed in the literature in great detail (Archer 2007; Bolton 2010). As it relates to reflection and the reflective process, it simply means we wish to understand how others perceive us and how our external environment affects us. Let's return to my memory of my first injection. If I had been reflexive within the reflective process, I would have also tried to analyse how the patient experienced me. This would have given me a different perspective, an added dimension – another way of viewing what happened. This would have resulted in a greater level of knowledge about myself that I could then have taken on board. Bolton shows us how, through reflective writing, we can develop the ability to view our experiences from another person's perspective.

Have a go at Exercise 5.5.

## Exercise 5.5: Being reflexive

In the space below, write down on the left-hand side your reflections on a recent experience you may have had in practice that impacted upon you. On the right-hand side, re-write the experience from the point of view of another person who was part of your experience.

| ***My perspective*** | ***The perspective of another*** |
|---|---|
| | |

Now consider what learning has taken place, having analysed the experience from not only your own perspective but also that of another.

Can you see how reflecting upon your experience from another person's perspective will offer a different dimension to your learning? By being reflexive in the reflective process we are:

> . . . finding strategies to question our own attitudes, thought processes, values, assumptions, prejudices and habitual actions, to strive to understand our complex role in relation to others.
> (Bolton 2010: 13)

Gaining that vital self-awareness in relation to how others perceive and experience you ensures not only a deeper level of reflection, especially when being mindful, but gives an added breadth of analysis.

Thus in essence, by being mindful in the reflective process, we are embodying the notion of reflection moment by moment. We are allowing it to become a more fluid, less mechanical process that ensures we are aware of ourselves at the time we are having or are about to have our experiences. The added element of reflexivity ensures that our reflection is more than one-dimensional, in that we not only get to know ourselves, but we also get to try and understand how other people view us.

By revisiting the extended description of reflection here, we can see where the ingredients of communication and mindfulness are situated:

> 'Reflection is an essential, engaging process that allows the reflector to frame and reframe their reality that is being experienced moment by moment. It requires us to utilize skills of communication, to become our own person-centred therapists, understanding ourselves in relation to experiences we are about to have, are having or have had, empathically and with accuracy, then stepping beyond the self and using this knowledge gained to understand how we may then have impacted on those around us.'

**Key points that can be taken from this chapter are:**

- When reflecting alone we need to become our own internal supervisor.
- Communication skills play a vital role in the reflective process of getting to know oneself.
- The use of Socratic dialogue helps us to ensure that the questioning we apply to get to know ourselves allows for honesty and a deeper level of learning.
- Empathic responding skills are supported by the empathic attitude discussed in Chapter 1.
- Empathic responding skills ensure we probe more deeply when we get to know ourselves and that we are accurate in our understanding of self.
- Being mindful ensures that reflection is not a mechanical process.
- Being mindful allows us to be acutely aware of ourselves moment to moment.
- The reflexivity involved in the reflective process allows us to view and understand ourselves from another person's perspective, ensuring reflection is multidimensional.

CHAPTER

# Being process-orientated and strategic

## Essential ingredient #9 – *Being process-orientated*

*'Reflection is not about the outcome/output, but about the process that takes place when reflecting. Reflection may not always be so smooth as to guarantee a definitive outcome. As much learning can take place from the process as can occur from the result.'*

(Adapted from Clarke 2014)

## Essential ingredient #10 – *Being strategic*

*'Reflecting is not a flippant, inconsequential recap of an event, but a deliberate, controlled, conscious consideration of an experience. The reflector must be cognisant that every decision they make as a result of reflection has a "ripple effect". The actions they take from the reflective process will not only impact upon the practitioner reflecting but on those around them.'*

(Adapted from Clarke 2014)

## Learning outcomes

By the end of this chapter, you will be able to:

- Understand how the notion of *process* underpins reflection
- Acknowledge that learning can take place during the process of reflecting
- Recognize that reflection is a strategic process
- Know that the decisions we put into practice as a result of reflecting will affect those around us and other areas of our lives
- Be accountable for the decisions made as a result of learning taken from reflection.

In the previous chapters, we have addressed eight of the ten essential ingredients for successful reflection. In looking at these eight essential ingredients in detail, we have learned how reflection is so much more than just examining what we have done well and what we have done not so well. We have learned that reflection is an analysis of ourselves, our thoughts, feelings, and behaviours, through and within the experiences we are going to have, have had or are having. We have discovered we do this in order to learn more about ourselves. To gain greater self-awareness is to be able to really understand 'me', to highlight any gaps in our ever-expanding knowledge and ultimately to enhance our levels of emotional intelligence in relation to knowing 'me', knowing how 'me' impacts on others, and how to use 'me' in the therapeutic relationship.

We have established that the eight ingredients we have discussed so far support our ability to reflect. We have found that the academic skills we use in our university work underpin our ability to be critical, to view our experiences analytically, and to question what we do, see, feel, and think. These academic skills allow us to recognize what our current knowledge is, and then use this to discover new knowledge.

We now know that our attitude – the bravery and courage we possess – is important in supporting the honesty required in the reflective process.

That our wanting to truly understand ourselves accurately, situating ourselves within a person-centred framework when reflecting, helps our empathy to be accurate, generating greater self-awareness. And finally, we have learned that this whole reflective process is underpinned by the way we communicate both with ourselves and with others who offer us guided reflection.

In this chapter, we examine our final two essential ingredients before addressing how to put all of what we have learned together as a package (like baking a cake), in order to engage in the reflective process both verbally and in written form. It is the purpose of this chapter to address the notions of *process* and *strategy*. We will focus here on understanding how the learning that occurs as a result of reflection doesn't simply materialize at the end of the process, but that we are able to learn throughout. We will see that through the process of reflection, by putting all of the ingredients into the mix, pervasive learning can occur. We will also see that reflection, and what we do with what we learn, needs to be strategic in order for it to become reflective practice, and whatever learning we put into place will also affect those around us.

Bolton (2010: 3) sees reflection as a 'state of mind, an on-going constituent of practice, not a technique or curriculum element'. In other words, it is a way of 'being', an embodiment of thinking and behaving in a particular way, a way that constantly encourages learning and the raising of emotional intelligence.

So with this in mind, let's take a look at our ninth essential ingredient – being process-orientated.

### Essential ingredient #9 – *Being process-orientated*

*'Reflection is not about the outcome/output, but about the process that takes place when reflecting. Reflection may not always be so smooth as to guarantee a definitive outcome. As much learning can take place from the process as can occur from the result.'*

(Adapted from Clarke 2014)

First, have a go at completing Exercise 6.1:

### Exercise 6.1: Defining process

In the space below, jot down what you think we mean when we use the word *process* in relation to reflection. What does this word mean to you?

I think that in terms of reflection, process means:

In thinking about the word 'process', I expect that you have suggested the steps taken to achieve a particular outcome, or the things we do to achieve a particular result. Those of you who have come across reflection as part of your programme of study may suggest that process in relation to reflection is to *describe* the experience, consider your *thoughts and feelings*, to *evaluate and analyse* this experience, and then decide on further *action* to be taken. The portrayal of process in this rigid manner (which is often as a result of being taught reflective models without being taught the underpinning philosophy of reflection itself) lacks the breadth and depth of understanding that we now know is the reflective process.

Let us recap for a moment what we have learned so far about reflection in the previous chapters. Taking this learning into account, process as it relates to reflection is about engaging in self-analysis; the deep contemplation of what we truly think and feel; the act of pondering these thoughts and feelings and relating this to our experiences; the mindful consideration of our behaviour; the recognition of our current knowledge; the seeking out of new knowledge; the act of getting to know ourselves; and the thoughtfulness and mindfulness that is required if we are to consider those around us and how they experience us. These are elements that we now know are an integral part of the process of reflecting.

To show how learning can take place through the process of engaging in an experience, let us look at two real-life examples. The first is a normal activity that many people will engage with at some point in their lives, while the second is an activity engaged in by all nursing students.

In the first example (Figure 6.1), the outcome is a cake. When you eat the cake, you almost certainly will consider its consistency, its taste, even the way it looks. You will learn from this what is aesthetically pleasing to you and what your taste buds respond to. What we are concerned with here though, is to show that one can learn from the *process* of baking the cake as well from the end result – the cake when baked. Look at Figure 6.1 and imagine that this is your first attempt at baking a cake. You will see some of the learning that has occurred if you reflect on-practice of the experience of baking. By the time the cake has been baked, you will have learned about ingredients, measurements, conversions, timings, and how to use an appliance. You will have learned about yourself: Did you enjoy baking? Did you have a sense of achievement? Satisfaction? You recognized gaps in your knowledge and you may have sought new knowledge.

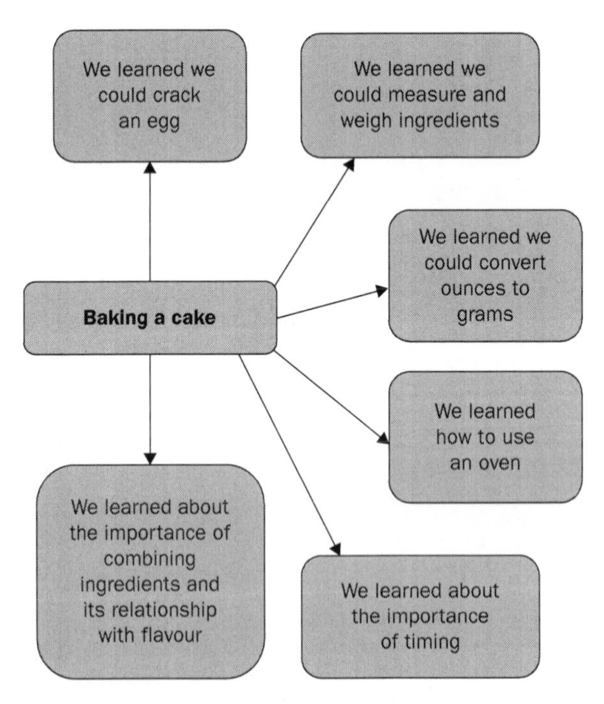


**Figure 6.1** Learning from the process: baking your first cake

Now let's look at our second example. The end result here is the giving of an injection (Figure 6.2). Reflecting on-practice, your learning may involve finding out that this procedure made you anxious and that you didn't particularly enjoy your first experience of it. You may come to realize that this is an intervention you need to practise. You may have learned that you need to brush up on your numeracy skills and that drug calculations can be quite complex.

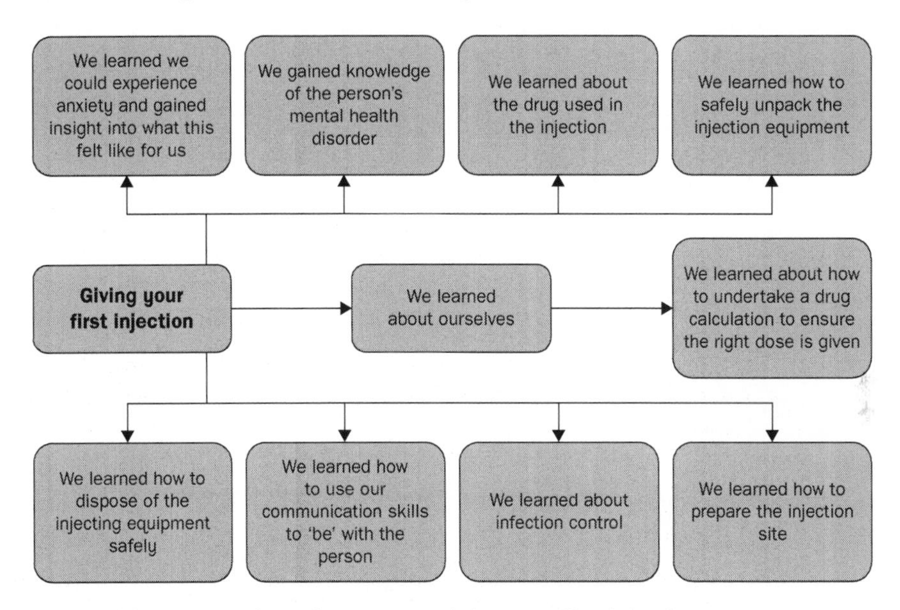


**Figure 6.2** Learning from the process: giving your first injection

However, the process of giving this injection gives us at least ten opportunities for learning. If in addition to reflection-on-action you pre-reflect, reflect in-action, and embody mindfulness before, during, and after, not only will you have learned about the injection, what it's for, the type of drug, and how to calculate the right dose, you will also have learned about yourself: about how you communicate with those around you and the person you gave the injection to; about your own insecurities and anxieties and how they affected you before, during, and after the experience, including the impact you had on those around you. As part of the process, you will have gained self-awareness and new knowledge – both theoretical and personal.

Learning taken from the process of reflection is not just an accumulation of facts, rather it is the kind of learning that makes a difference to your behaviour, the course of action you choose to take in the future, your attitudes and your personality. Carl Rogers, who we encountered in earlier chapters, refers to this type of learning as pervasive learning that is not just an accumulation of knowledge, but knowledge that interpenetrates with every portion of our existence (Rogers 1967). When Rogers wrote about learning that can take place in the helping relationship, and more specifically within psychotherapy, he advised us of the following key areas for gaining knowledge:

- The person sees themselves differently.
- They accept themselves and their feelings more fully.
- They become more self-confident and self-directing.
- They become more the person they would like to be.
- They become more flexible, less rigid in their perceptions.
- They adopt more realistic goals for themselves.
- They behave in a more mature fashion.
- They change maladjusted behaviours.
- They become more accepting of others.
- They become more open to the evidence, both to what is going on outside themselves and what is going on inside themselves.
- They change in basic personality characteristics, in constructive ways.

Rogers wrote about these key areas in 1967, but it is clear that these remain just as relevant to us today. This is the incredible learning that can occur through the reflective process. So for those of you who remain to be convinced about the learning that can take place, even having read the previous chapters, we will take a closer look at what these key areas can mean when reflecting. Box 6.1 details how these key areas and the reflective process intertwine.

We can see here the absolute potential for the pervasive learning that Rogers' key areas can foster in the process of reflection. Ultimately, these key areas relate to a learning about ourselves that allows us to become the person we want to be, it allows us to truly understand ourselves so we can adjust our behaviours if we need to. This type of learning allows us to achieve a level of emotional intelligence that facilitates understanding of the relationship we have with our external environment, and an understanding of those around us in a way that supports our acceptance of and recognition of our impact on others. This pervasive learning is the knowledge and wisdom we are endeavouring to achieve through the process of

## Box 6.1: Rogers' key areas of pervasive learning and their relationship with the reflective process

| *Key area* | *Description* |
|---|---|
| The person sees themselves differently | Reflection allows us to frame and reframe our experiences, it allows us to see the experience from a different perspective, and can provide us with new meanings. Being mindful and reflexive ensures we try and view how others perceive us in our experience and how we may impact upon them. As a result, we understand our experience from a number of different angles, which may allow us to see ourselves differently from first envisaged. |
| They accept themselves and their feelings more fully | The process of reflection teaches us that to really be honest with ourselves about how we think and feel, to gain that accurate empathy, we need to be non-judgemental. To really understand ourselves, we adopt a non-judgemental stance that enables true acceptance of what we would describe as 'me' or 'I'. |
| They become more self-confident and self-directing | The process of reflecting allows us to practise honesty. This honesty supports the revealing of what we do and don't know. The act of engaging with what we don't know allows us to take action and to fill those gaps in our knowledge. We ultimately become more practised and therefore more comfortable with our ability to know what we do and don't know, and to source new knowledge. Increased capability increases self-confidence. |
| They become more the person they would like to be | The process of reflection wants us to use our current self-awareness to get to know ourselves more deeply, generating deeper levels of self-awareness. This process means that we can recognize what we like and dislike about ourselves and as a result of the process we can make transformative changes to be more of the person we ultimately see ourselves to be. |
| They become more flexible, less rigid in their perceptions | The process of reflection, learning to be reflexive and mindful, helps us to realize that there is more than one view of a situation. In knowing that there is more than one way to perceive an experience and by knowing how others see us and what our impact is on them, we can learn to freely acknowledge and accept other perceptions and thus choose to be less rigid. |

*(Continued)*

**Box 6.1: (continued)**

| *Key area* | *Description* |
|---|---|
| They adopt more realistic goals for themselves | Engaging in the process of reflection persuades us to analyse and evaluate our experiences. If we do this openly and honestly, we can view our experiences and the realness of them. We can determine if the expectations we have of ourselves are reasonable. Through analysis and evaluation, we can alter and adapt our expectations and goals. This part of the process helps us to not have unrealistic views of life as well as allowing us to expand our horizons if our goals and views are too narrow. |
| They behave in a more mature fashion | The process of reflection is about learning, not just about the mechanics of nursing interventions but about ourselves. In the process of learning we become more emotionally mature, which leads to a greater emotional intelligence. This emotional intelligence can support not only professional practice, where we have greater understanding of how we are in the therapeutic relationship, but also in our personal lives, in the relationships we have with ourselves and family and friends. We can therefore behave and experience life in a more controlled, understood, and mature way. |
| They change maladjusted behaviours | The insight we gain into ourselves from the process of reflection ensures we can understand our behaviour and why we think and feel the way we do. This understanding also means we get to know how we impact on those around us. In essence, we get to know what works for us and what doesn't work. The more mature we become as a result of the process gives us the confidence to really acknowledge what works and allows us to change the behaviour, thoughts, and feelings that are not so useful to us. |
| They become more accepting of others | In developing our ability to view our experiences from many different perspectives, we are able to see multiple realities. That our reality is just that, our reality, and others can experience our reality quite differently. The process teaches us to accept the different perspectives and to learn from this. As a result, we can choose to become more accepting of others because we learn that in our acceptance, we don't always need to agree. |

**Box 6.1: (continued)**

| *Key area* | *Description* |
|---|---|
| They become more open to the evidence, both to what is going on outside themselves, and to what is going on inside of themselves | The process of reflection is all about understanding what is going on within ourselves and how we are impacted upon by our external environment. But the process of reflection teaches us to not just understand, but to be open to sourcing new knowledge. The process allows us to recognize the gaps we have in our knowledge and to be open to the evidence that could possibly fill those gaps. |
| They change in basic personality characteristics, in constructive ways | We know from previous chapters about the transformative nature of change that can occur within the reflective process. Through the process of reflection we can learn about ourselves if we truly engage. If we truly engage and are open to the learning, we can change parts of who we are should we wish to do so. This change is not always conscious but the process can lead to subtle change for the better. |

reflecting for ourselves. As trainee nurses, you will endeavour to impart this to your service users, supporting them so that their own learning can help them to live their lives to their own unique potential.

Take a look at the key areas again. What do you think of the descriptions I have provided of the relationship each area has with the process of reflection? Are there any areas that you would add?

Adding to our discussion on process and learning, Jayne Dalley also recognizes that the process of reflection can be as important as the outcome depending on the context within which we are reflecting. She believes that the purpose of reflection is also about the acquisition of skills and learning during the actual process:

> Whether the purpose is seeking the outcomes of reflection or seeking the development of reflective skills *per se*. Is the outcome considered more important? Or is the process by which that outcome is arrived at considered the more important?
>
> (Dalley 2009: 19)

Consider the following two examples. These examples demonstrate the point at which two different branches of nursing might learn from reflection.

1 The first is of an adult nurse reflecting on why her patient is not responding to their prescribed dose of insulin. The nurse may not place much importance on the process of reflection; she may be more interested in an answer to this particular question, which is the 'outcome'.
2 A mental health nurse may be reflecting upon why he responded and felt a certain way about a particular patient. To this nurse, the process of reflection – getting to know himself, being mindful, reflexive, processing thoughts and feelings in the reflective process, going through Rogers' key areas – may be just as important if not more so than answering a question that may not be answerable.

Here we can see two purposes to reflection. The first is outcome driven, the second process driven. The adult nurse may perceive that learning only takes place when reflecting to produce an outcome to an event, which is very different to the mental health nurse who perceives that learning takes place during the process of reflecting. Neither is incorrect; however, the adult nurse needs to realize that as much can be learnt during the process as from the outcome (if there is an outcome).

It is important to note that there may not always be an outcome as a result of reflection, but there will always be a process that learning can be taken from. This is similar to our examination of critical analysis in earlier chapters, in that there may not always be critique but there will be analysis to form the basis of learning. The adult nurse above might learn from the process of reflecting in relation to the insulin question, to ensure that her reflection is more than just critical incident analysis.

So let's give it a try. Have a look at Exercise 6.2.

## Exercise 6.2: Learning from the process

First, consider an experience that had a marked impact on you. Maybe an experience from one of your clinical placements, or an experience you had outside university. Then, in the space below, provide a brief description of the experience before breaking that experience down into sections or stages, as in Figures 6.1 and 6.2. Consider each section in turn and write down the learning you took from it (this is the process).

Next, consider the experience as a whole and jot down the overall learning taken from the experience (this is the outcome). While undertaking this exercise, bear in mind the other essential ingredients for successful reflection, and underpin this with Rogers' key areas of pervasive learning. Put those ingredients into action when undertaking this exercise.

| ***Brief description of the experience*** | ***Process sections*** | ***Learning taken from each section*** | ***Learning as a result of the overall outcome*** |
|---|---|---|---|
| | | | |

What you are doing here is teaching yourself how to reflect – putting all the previous ingredients into practice to show how reflection is a process and how learning can be taken from this process. You should learn as much from breaking down the experience and reflecting on the process of the experience as you do from reflecting on the outcome.

If we revisit the extended description of reflection, we can see where this ingredient is situated.

'Reflection is an essential, engaging process that allows the reflector to frame and reframe their reality that is being experienced moment by moment.'

## Being strategic

Let's now take a look at our tenth and final essential ingredient for successful reflection – being strategic.

## Essential ingredient #10 – *Being strategic*

*'Reflecting is not a flippant, inconsequential recap of an event, but a deliberate, controlled, conscious consideration of an experience. The reflector must be cognisant that every decision they make as a result of reflection has a "ripple effect". The actions they take from the reflective process will not only impact upon the practitioner reflecting but on those around them.'*

(Adapted from Clarke 2014)

This ingredient is about recognizing that reflection is *strategic* – that it is not an ad hoc recollection of events, or a thoughtless consideration of how we are behaving. Reflection is very meaningful and involves deliberate, thoughtful consideration of our experiences. Even reflecting in the moment where we are mindful is a conscious, intentional consideration of who we are, what we are, and how we are. During your training, you have likely been introduced to reflective models and cycles, which provide a framework within which to reflect. These models (for example, those of Borton, Gibbs, Atkins, and Murphy) recognize the strategic nature of reflection and the importance of ensuring the reflector is supported during the process. However, as I noted earlier, these models can be used incorrectly if the underpinning philosophy of reflection is not understood. Because of this, I have dedicated a whole chapter to reflective models and cycles, so that you can learn how to use them appropriately.

### Technical reflection

In addition to reflective models, writers on reflection have also alluded to the strategic nature of reflection. Beverly Taylor (2000) has referred to the notion of *technical reflection*, which she sees as a level of reflection that requires nurses to think critically and reason scientifically about what they have learned in the reflective process so that they can critique and adjust current behaviours/ways of working when necessary. Technical reflection is deliberate and strategic and is about influencing clinical practice. This type of reflection is outcome driven and more akin to critical incident analysis whereby we deliberately consider the mechanics of interventions in the clinical area, and relate our learning to the current evidence base. However, technical reflection is still underpinned by the information we have discussed in previous chapters, in particular the academic skills of analysis and critique and sourcing knowledge.

As you are now aware, even analysis and critique are strategic in their conscious and measured consideration of events in light of the evidence. So Taylor (2000), having been influenced by authors such as Bandman and Bandman (1995) and Van Hooft et al. (1995), refers to technical reflection as the scientific reasoning and function of a critical thinker underpinned by the problem-solving steps of the nursing process (Wilkinson 1996). Implementing the process of technical reflection involves developing an argument by analysing the issues and assumptions managing the situation, planning and assessing, and evaluating the problem in light of all the information gained through the process of technical reflection. Overall, this is not at all dissimilar to the reflective process, but with more focus potentially on the outcome. Thus, if we engage in Taylor's idea of technical reflection, the process will be undertaken in a thoughtful, considered, and strategic manner. Technical reflection highlights the deliberate process undertaken in order to ensure learning takes place when reflecting.

In writing about reflection, Van Manen (1995) broke the process down into four elements demonstrating how strategic reflection can be. Box 6.2 provides a commentary on each of these four elements.

We can clearly see there are four very separate stages that are mindfully engaged with during the reflective process, further supporting the first part of essential ingredient #10:

'Reflecting is not a flippant, inconsequential recap of an event, but a deliberate, controlled, conscious consideration of an experience.'

We can also see how these stages align very closely with all the other ingredients in previous chapters.

Let us take a look now at the second part of the ingredient that is being strategic.

## Box 6.2: The four elements of reflection

| *Element* | *Description* |
|---|---|
| **Anticipatory** | Before engaging in a task, the reflector is required to think about possible actions, interventions, and probable outcomes, often referred to as pre-reflection. |
| **Active** | The reflector is able to maintain and promote awareness of what they are doing at any given time. This requires the reflector to be conscious of what they are doing at the time they are doing it. |
| **Mindful** | The reflector has developed and is developing the capacity to be actively reflective and thoughtful during the experiences that they are encountering, sometimes referred to as 'thinking on the job' or reflecting on-action. |
| **Recollective** | Having thought about the experience to be encountered, the reflector becomes consciously aware during the experience, reflects at the time of the experience, and is able to consider and evaluate the experience by addressing the success of any outcome. |

Source: Adapted from Van Manen (1995).

'The reflector must be cognisant that every decision they make as a result of reflection has a "ripple effect". The actions they take from the reflective process will not only impact upon the practitioner reflecting but on those around them.'

This second part requires us not only to recognize that reflection is a strategic process, even when there isn't an outcome, but that our action based on the learning gained in the reflective process can have an a wider audience, not just ourselves.

In Chapter 5, where we addressed mindfulness, we learned that in the reflective process we must consider the impact our experiences have on those around us. We learned that reflection is more than just self-indulgent rumination – that learning about ourselves can be enhanced if we consider the impact our behaviour (including our thoughts and feelings) has on others. Being strategic requires us to take this a step further. In being strategic in the process, we need to consider the impact any action or decision we make as a result of the reflective process might have on those around us. Thus, not just reflecting on how we affect people during our experiences but also on the effect we can have on people following the experience and reflection. This ingredient, therefore, requires us to think strategically about what we do with the learning before we take any kind of action; that is, consider the likely impact of our actions – both on ourselves and others.

Can you remember a time when you made a decision to change your approach? Do you remember applying thoughtful consideration to the implications your approach might have had on your environment and those around you? Did you consider the 'ripple effect' or the knock-on effect your approach might have had?

Let's look at a situation you may come across as a senior nurse/ward manager to understand this notion of the ripple effect.

*Scenario 6.1*

You have reflected diligently and from the learning that has taken place you have decided to implement a change in practice on your ward. You decide to send all the ward staff on a three-day drug and alcohol training programme that occurs once a year, at a cost of £1000 per person. Figure 6.3 highlights the potential impact of sending all the staff on this training course. Can you think of any other ways in which this training could have a wider impact, or create a ripple effect?

A reflective manager would consider and analyse in the reflective process the impact this course of action might have before it is implemented. If the ripple effect were to result in some negative outcome, the course of action ought to be adapted.

Having now looked at all ten ingredients for successful reflection, it is clear that reflection is a deliberate and strategic process. All potential learning can result in action being taken, action that can have an impact on others not just the reflector.

If we revisit the new, extended description of reflection, we can see where these two ingredients are situated. Unlike the previous

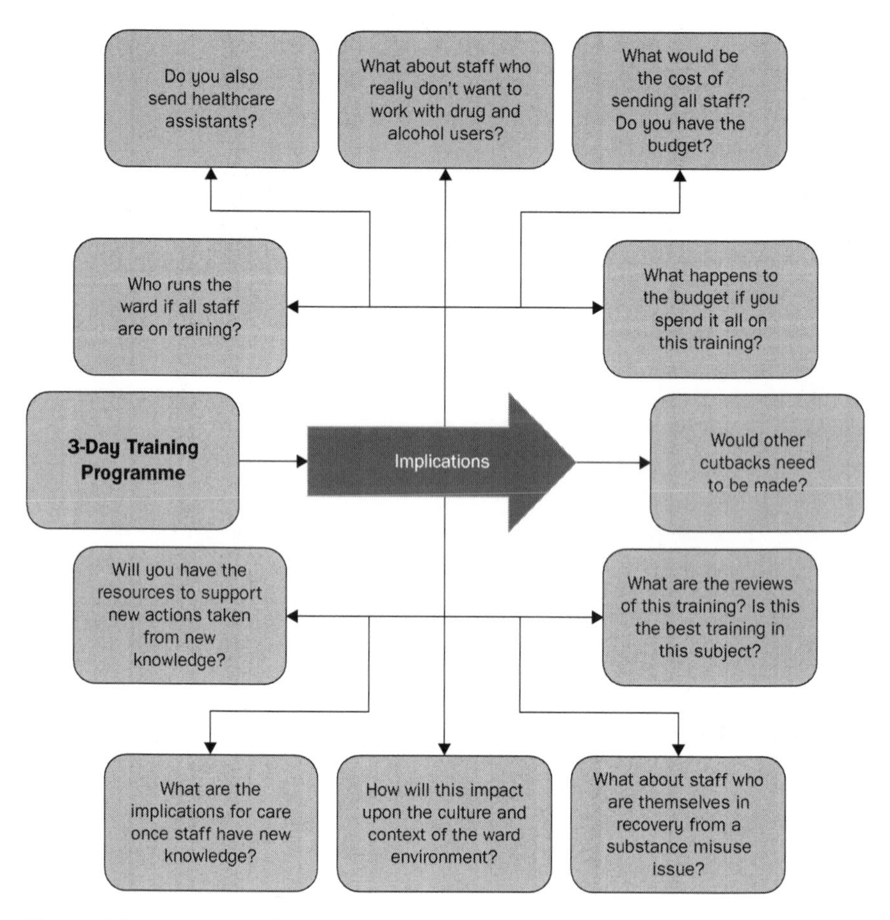


**Figure 6.3** The ripple effect

ingredients, however, being process-orientated and strategic underpins the whole of the extended description:

## A new, extended description of reflection

'Reflection is an essential, engaging process that allows the reflector to frame and reframe their reality that is being experienced moment by moment. It requires us to utilize skills of communication, to become our own person-centred therapists, understanding ourselves in relation to experiences we are about to have, are having or have had, empathically and with accuracy, then stepping beyond the self and using this knowledge gained to understand how we may then have impacted on those around us. For this process to bear fruit, we must leave arrogance and complacency at the door, be kind and compassionate, offering ourselves unconditional positive regard, be actively engaged in mindfulness, consciously aware of the self in the moment, open to learning and sourcing new knowledge if the knowledge is not already known to us, using the new knowledge gained to develop ourselves personally and professionally in a critically analytical manner. When fully engaged in the reflective process, the experience can be humbling as we realize we are not perhaps what we assumed ourselves to be, yet also rewarding as we confirm that our best may have at that time been good enough.'

**Key points that can be taken from this chapter are:**

- The notion of process underpins our reflection.
- Just as much learning can occur from the process of engaging in reflection as can by understanding the outcome.
- The learning taken from the process is a pervasive learning that ensures a deep level of understanding.
- Reflection is a strategic, deliberate, and considered process.
- Our actions as a result of reflection affect more than just ourselves.

CHAPTER

# Frameworks for reflection

## Learning outcomes

By the end of this chapter, you will be able to:

- Understand the purpose of reflective frameworks
- Make an informed decision as to the usefulness of the different frameworks in supporting your engagement with reflection
- Determine which of the reflective frameworks presented in this chapter align most closely with the way you reflect
- Use a reflective framework appropriately in supporting the reflective process
- Understand how reflective frameworks are underpinned by the extended description of reflection and the ten essential ingredients
- Source other reflective frameworks not considered here.

The previous chapters have taught us everything we need to now know about reflection to be able to get on and reflect. We have learned that by supporting our understanding of reflection with the extended description and utilizing the ten essential ingredients in combination, we have all that we need to reflect. In understanding these ten ingredients and how they interconnect and support one another, we now know what reflection is, its purpose, its usefulness both professionally and personally, and quite simply how to do it. We have also come to understand that the learning that occurs as a result of reflection begins during the process and is not just a product of the outcome.

A number of reflective cycles and models have been developed by researchers, academics, and professionals working in the caring professions. For our purposes, we shall refer to these cycles and models as frameworks. The purpose of these frameworks is to support us in our endeavours to reflect. The frameworks offer us a structure within which to reflect, within which to employ or mix up our ingredients so that we can reflect effectively. Frameworks are especially useful for the novice reflector until reflection becomes second nature. However, there is no one correct framework to use, no official requirement to use a framework, and our ten essential ingredients can be used with or without one. As mentioned earlier in this book, frameworks are not helpful if you do not understand the notion of reflection first. Using a reflective framework before you understand reflection is like putting the cart before the horse, or trying to drive a car without understanding the principles of driving. Reflective frameworks can also be overlaid – that is, we can use more than one at a time. But they are not, in my opinion, essay structures, a view I shall explain later.

This chapter will focus on some of the more common frameworks that you may already have heard about and that can be used to support your reflection. We have met some of these in previous chapters but we shall address them again in order to understand how we can use them in the reflective process. We will look at how these frameworks can underpin our reflection and support us in breaking down our experiences so we can put into action the ten essential ingredients.

**But remember, there is no one right way to reflect, no one correct framework to use. As long as you adopt the ten essential ingredients, you will be able to reflect in whatever mode whenever you wish.**

### Exercise 7.1: Naming reflective frameworks

In the space below, jot down any reflective frameworks (models/cycles) you have heard of.

I am aware of the following reflective frameworks:

Of the reflective frameworks you have listed, which one(s) have you used? What were your thoughts on this framework? Why did you use this particular one?

We will revisit this exercise later to determine if your opinions on the frameworks have altered after reading the chapter.

## David A. Kolb's experiential learning cycle

Before we delve deeper into reflective frameworks, we need to acknowledge the work of David A. Kolb. Kolb, an educational theorist, is a key promoter of learning by doing, and his work has often been perceived as 'presenting the foundations for learning by doing' (Jasper 2003: 3). Kolb perceived that we learn from what we live through, and that learning takes place when we reflect on and break down the experiences we have had: 'Learning is the process whereby knowledge is created through the transformation of experience' (Kolb 1984: 38).

Kolb developed the *experiential learning cycle*, which considers that reflecting on experience (on-action) is an integral part of the way in which we learn. It proposes that the purpose of reflection on experience is to stimulate further inquiry or study and, in doing so, generate new cycles of meaningful activity (further experiences), in turn aimed at creating new knowledge. Kolb (1984) stated that the development of cognitive, intellectual, and practical skills is a product of activity.

Figure 7.1 is a depiction of Kolb's experiential learning cycle. There are four separate and distinctive areas. These areas need to be encountered for learning to take place and the cyclical nature is the key to moving forwards. Kolb draws attention to the reflective aspect of the cycle – that in order to learn, we need to have experiences, but we then need to recall those experiences and reflect on them. Through reflection and analysis of what we experience, we learn new knowledge and ground current knowledge. Reflection can give rise to a new idea or a modification of an existing abstract concept. Kolb proposes we then apply what we have learned to the world around us by taking some form of action.

Although reflection is part of Kolb's experiential learning cycle, I would argue that this is not a reflective cycle *per se*, but a cycle that

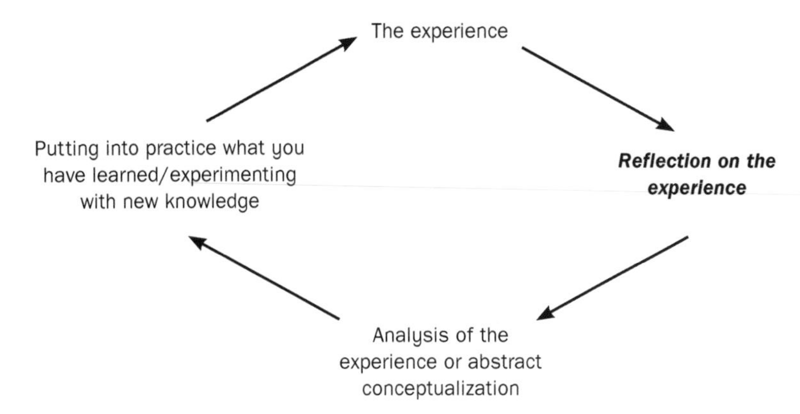


**Figure 7.1** Experiential learning cycle

demonstrates reflection as being an integral part of the learning process. Kolb's experiential learning cycle has, however, helped give rise to the various reflective frameworks that have emerged over the years. These reflective frameworks provide structure for stage 2 of Kolb's cycle – *reflection*. As novice reflectors, you need to recognize that this is a cycle of learning, not a framework within which to reflect.

Over the years, various supporters of reflection and reflective practice have devised and advocated a range of models to guide and develop the practice of, in the main, reflection-on-action. Key supporters of models for reflection and learning include Borton (1970), Gibbs (1988), Atkins and Murphy (1994), Rolfe et al. (2001), and Johns (2004). We will now take a brief look at the most common frameworks for reflection, ones that you may have already come across as part of your studies.

## Gibbs' reflective framework

Let us first look at a framework we have covered previously, Gibbs' (1988) reflective framework. Over the years, Gibbs' reflective framework has achieved great acclaim. Jasper (2003) has said that it would be difficult to find a textbook or paper written on reflection that does not at some point refer to Gibbs, or draw from his work in some way. So let us take a closer look at this cycle and what the stages require.

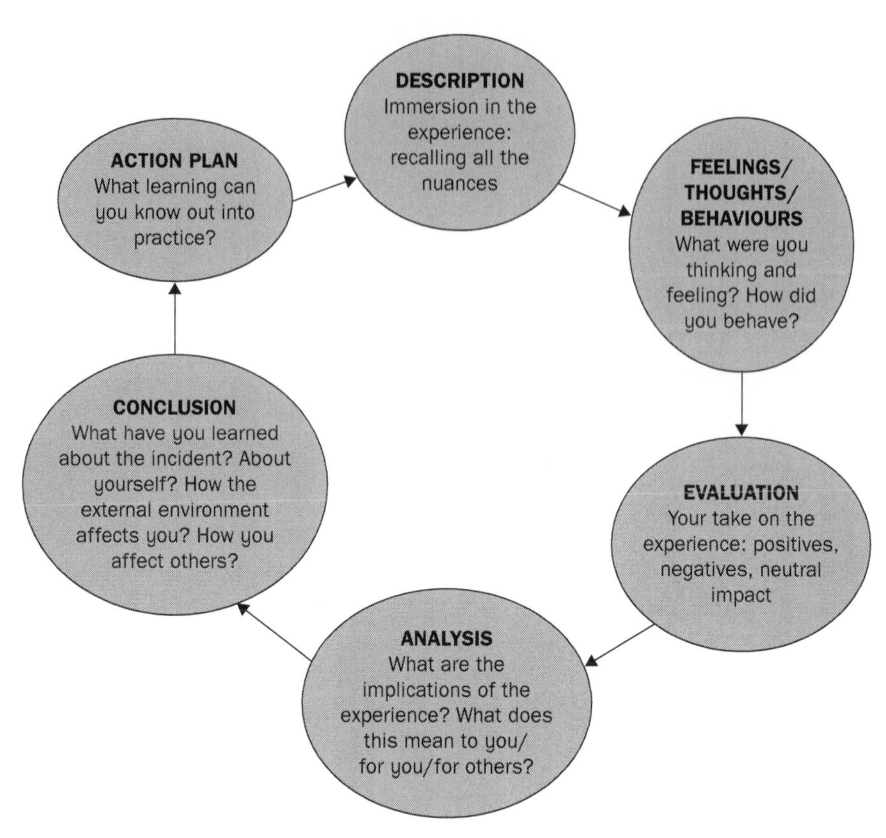


**Figure 7.2** Gibbs' reflective framework
Source: Adapted from Gibbs (1988).

### *Stage 1: Description of the event*

Here, we consider or think about an experience or event we wish to reflect upon. We can do this by telling another person what happened, writing down what happened, or we can recall the experience in our own mind. The aim here is to recall what impacted upon us, what resonated with us so that we have something to analyse and reflect upon.

This does not need to be a lengthy description of the experience, just a summary of a few sentences. When you are asked to undertake a reflective writing task, you may well be given a 2000 word limit. If you are, take care not to use the first 1500 words describing what happened, leaving yourself a few words to truly explore the remaining stages.

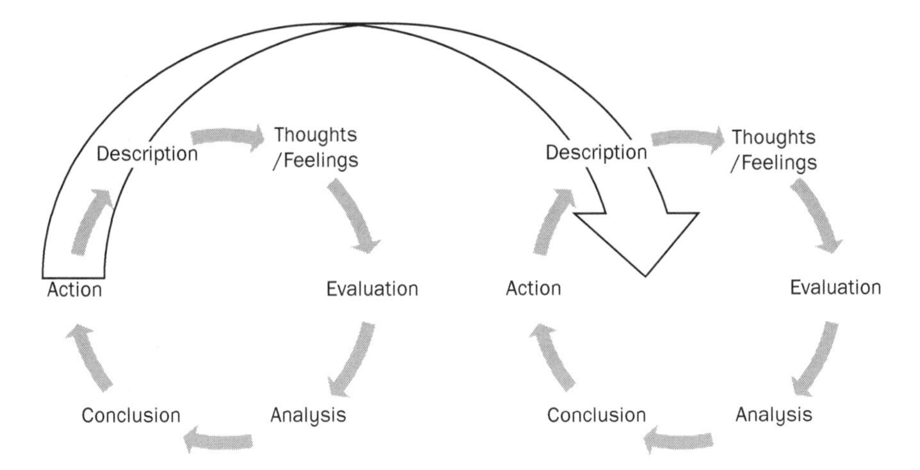


**Figure 7.3** The cyclical nature of Gibbs' framework

Figure 7.3 shows the cyclical nature of Gibbs' framework. Following a brief description, we can go through all of the stages, then after the action stage we can start the whole process once again with further description about the experience, and so on. So instead of writing a lengthy description and missing opportunities for analysis and understanding, provide a short description before spending the rest of your time on the next five stages of the cycle, then repeat.

### *Stage 2: Thoughts and feelings*

It is at this stage that we consider carefully the brief description and access our true thoughts and feelings about what occurred. We need to access the thoughts and feelings in relation to the description we have just given. This enables us to remain focused on what we are reflecting on. But remember through all of this we need to employ the ten essential ingredients, especially those introduced in Chapters 3 and 4: attitudinal qualities and self-awareness, and being person-centred and empathic. Bringing into play the essential ingredients allows us to be truly honest about our experience and our perception of it.

### *Stage 3: Evaluation*

This is where we judge what we have experienced in the brief description. We give it a value or a perception. Did we like it? Was it good? Is it what we wanted to experience and think and feel? What is our judgement of stages 1 and 2? Chapter 6 – being process-orientated and strategic – comes into play here. It is important to remember that this stage is much more than simply identifying what was good or bad. Such language denotes a lack of depth and maturity to the understanding that will underpin our knowledge at this stage. It could be suggested that answering what was good or bad about an experience requires very little thought. It directs us towards a descriptive interpretation of events that is reliant upon the recall of superficial knowledge from memory rather than provoking a more sophisticated way of remembering the event.

### *Stage 4: Analysis*

This is the stage when we get into the real detail. We now start to address the implications of the first three stages. At this stage, we really want to understand the description, the thoughts/feelings, and the evaluation. This is where Chapters 2 (academic skills and knowledge), 4 (being person-centred and empathic), and 5 (communication and mindfulness) come into play. What we learned in these three chapters will bolster our ability to ask questions of our experience, ensuring we achieve that deep level of understanding that will enhance our emotional intelligence.

I would suggest that, unlike in Gibbs' cycle, before proceeding to stage 5, we repeat stage 3 – evaluation. Before concluding, it's important to evaluate the analysis of the experience. We need to consolidate the analysis through evaluation, then draw conclusions from the evaluation before taking action.

### *Stage 5: Conclusion*

Having explored our experience from different angles and looked at the implications of our thoughts and feelings, having evaluated the learning, we can now draw conclusions about what we have learned. This is where we pull all the analysis together and ask questions of what we have learned. This is where we consolidate.

### *Stage 6: Action*

The action stage is where we do something with the learning that has taken place. This ensures that our reflection becomes reflective practice. This stage requires us to consider what would happen if we encountered the experience again, whether we do things differently. Also, we need to consider here what we can do with the learning that has occurred in other areas and aspects of our lives.

Using the ten essential ingredients to underpin how we engage with Gibbs' framework encourages us to remember and consider the experience in a more sophisticated manner. Rolfe (2011) suggested that Gibbs' framework uses cues that are general and unspecific, and that this generic feel could be advantageous to some, but to the novice practitioner it may be considered too vague and therefore unhelpful. The ten essential ingredients support the depth of exploration and analysis that the verbal cues that Gibbs provide us with do not.

Let's now turn to another widely used framework. Although it has fewer stages, it is similar to that of Gibbs in what it asks us to do in the reflective process.

## Borton's framework for reflection

Borton's (1970) framework offers us a model with the same aspects as Gibbs but with fewer stages. It is a framework that recognizes the need for healthcare practitioners to access a reflective structure immediately and to be able to reflect effectively in the real world of practice. Borton's framework is given structure by three basic questions.

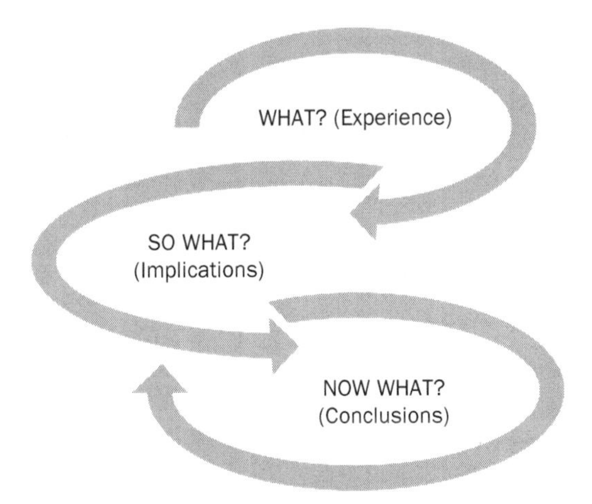


**Figure 7.4** Borton's framework for reflection

Source: Adapted from Borton (1970).

This framework, although simple, can be used on its own or in a highly analytical manner by the experienced reflector who underpins the framework with our ten essential ingredients.

Here there are three interconnecting stages. This is a developmental framework, as the three stages not only interlink but follow on from one another. Borton asks us to consider:

- *What?*
- *So what?* and
- *Now what?*

Let's take a closer look at the meaning of these.

### What?

The *What?* stage combines the first two stages of Gibbs (1988): *description* and *feelings*. At this point, we need to engage with identifying, recalling, and describing the experience. We also need to consider our thoughts and feelings.

### So what?

The *So what?* stage combines the third, fourth, and fifth aspects of Gibbs: *evaluation*, *analysis*, and *conclusion*. This stage requires us to break down the experience and to try to understand ourselves within the experience. We break down the description and try to make sense of what happened. This is where we gain enough information about the experience and understanding of ourselves to move onto to the next and final part of Borton's framework.

### Now what?

The *Now what?* stage is the equivalent of Gibbs' final stage of *action*. This is where we put into practice what we have learned. We consider the learning that has taken place during the first two stages and we develop an action point or points that enable us to use the learning or develop on from the learning that has occurred.

### A comparison of Gibbs and Borton

Although the above two frameworks are similar to one another, that of Borton suggests a simplicity about reflection that could be misleading. To use these two models appropriately and to gain the depth of understanding required from the reflective process, we need to understand reflection and its purpose and to use the ten essential ingredients to underpin the reflection conducted within both frameworks.

Before moving on, have a go at the following exercise.

## Exercise 7.3: What questions would you ask yourself?

In the space below, jot down the kinds of questions you might ask yourself in each of the stages when using one or other of these two reflective frameworks. Gibbs' stages have been grouped under the three stages of Borton's model.

| ***Borton*** | *What?* | *So what?* | *Now what?* |
|---|---|---|---|
| ***Gibbs*** | *Description Thoughts and feelings* | *Evaluation Analysis Conclusion* | *Action* |
| **What questions would you ask yourself?** | | | |

Some of the questions you may have come up with are:

**What?/Description/Thoughts and feelings:**

- What happened?
- What did I experience?
- What was I doing?
- How was I behaving?
- What was I thinking, feeling?
- What were others doing?

**So what?/Evaluation/Analysis/Conclusion:**

- Why do I think I behaved in the way that I did?
- What do I need to know more of to understand this better?

- Why do I think I felt the way I did?
- What do I need to understand about the thought I had?
- How did those around me impact on me and I on them?

**Now what?/Action:**

- What do I need to do with this information?
- Do I need to alter something about myself?
- Do I need to review my practice?

It is clear from both of these frameworks, as a result of the final stages, that what we are trying to do here is affect practice, or invoke a change in the way we do something, or react to and engage with situations. These models do support us in ensuring our reflection becomes reflective practice. Both models are simplistic, so we cannot let them detract from the complexity of what is reflection. Ensuring we underpin our use of reflective models with the extended description of reflection, the ten essential ingredients will support us in staying true to the complex nature of the reflective process and ensure our reflection is more than just a vivid recall of events.

## Rolfe's framework for reflexive practice

In recognition of the more widespread use of Borton's framework within healthcare and nursing programmes, and also in recognition of its simplicity, Rolfe et al. (2001) developed and extended this framework by devising further questions for the reflector to ask him or herself to give more substance to the three basic stages. This is extremely helpful, especially for nurses starting out on their reflective journey.

As we can see in Box 7.1, Rolfe et al (2001) have expanded on Borton's model by incorporating the cyclical nature of Gibbs (1988) and the greater detail it encapsulates, together with some of the Socratic dialogue we met in Chapter 5 from Johns' (2004) model of structured reflection. I have further adapted the dialogue in the framework to make it more accessible for students and to ensure that there is no assumption that the experience being reflected upon is always a negative one. Here we have an example of what we came across earlier, an overlaying or a combination of frameworks. Rolfe at al. (2001) have also referred to this as a *reflexive* framework rather

## Box 7.1: A framework for reflexive practice

| ***Descriptive level of reflection*** | ***Theory- and knowledge-building level of reflection*** | ***Action-orientated level of reflection*** |
|---|---|---|
| | | |
| **What?** | So what? | Now what? |
| **. . . is the nature of the problem?**<br>**. . . was my role and behaviour in the situation?**<br>**. . . did I want the outcome to be?**<br>**. . . did I do?**<br>**. . . was the response of those around me, my mentor, my patient, the family?**<br>**. . . were the implications for those involved?**<br>**. . . feelings did I have?**<br>**. . . feelings do I think others had?**<br>**. . . was positive/ negative/ ambivalent about the experience?** | . . . have I learned about:<br>• myself<br>• my behaviour<br>• others<br>• the experience?<br>. . . how did my thoughts/feelings impact on my behaviour?<br>. . . what evidence did I need to immerse myself in?<br>. . . potentially could I have done to improve the experience?<br>. . . is my understanding of this experience?<br>. . . else has arisen as a result of this experience? | . . . do I need to do in order to:<br>• improve on a similar experience?<br>• improve my care delivery?<br>• ensure a negative situation does not re-occur?<br>• enhance my feelings of wellbeing?<br>• have more positive experiences?<br>• etc., etc.?<br>. . . wider issues need to be considered if this action is to be successful?<br>. . . might be the implications of this action? |

Source: Adapted from Rolfe et al. (2001), cited in Jasper (2003: 101).

than a reflective framework because the questions asked mean we take action that allows us to *change* the experience, rather than just learn from it. The action we take means that we don't repeat the same experience twice; thus we can produce a new situation. Jasper (2003) has suggested that the reflexive practitioner is someone who is in a continuous state of reflective practice, learning from experiences, and as a result is able to change their experiences as they experience them. If you remember, this was referred to in previous chapters as reflecting in-action and mindfulness.

What do you think of Rolfe's framework? Do you think that, with the knowledge you now have about reflection and equipped with the ten essential ingredients for successful reflection, this would be a useful framework for you? Looking at the questions/cues it asks us to use, do you think the framework has missed any areas?

Within the university setting, it is often the case that the manner in which you are asked to reflect as a nursing student is by way of presentation and/or written assignment. You are often expected to reflect alone when writing your reflective assignments or preparing for reflective presentations and it could be that your only guide or support in the reflective process is one of the frameworks discussed in this chapter. As I have already said, they enable to a certain extent a strategic approach to what could be a rather random exercise, very useful if you are a novice reflector. However, for the novice or even experienced reflector, the terminology may not be overly helpful in the development of reflective skills and in aiding the complex dialogue we need to have with ourselves during the reflective process. So, before we consider what we have learned from understanding reflective frameworks, let's take a look at one further reflective framework that you may have already come across.

## Atkins and Murphy's framework for reflection

As you can see from Figure 7.5, this framework utilizes expressions that may not be as easy to understand as some of the other ones we have looked at. For example, take the term 'salient feelings': it is unlikely that it will be clear to all novice reflectors what 'salient' means – noticeable or leading. In the first stage of this framework when we recall the experience, we are immediately asked to become aware of what we were uncomfortable with and to address the negativity of what occurred. There is an assumption here that we are reflecting because we had a bad experience. But we now know that we can reflect and learn just as much from the positive experiences we have, and we also know that experiences can generate positive, negative, and even ambivalent thoughts and feelings.

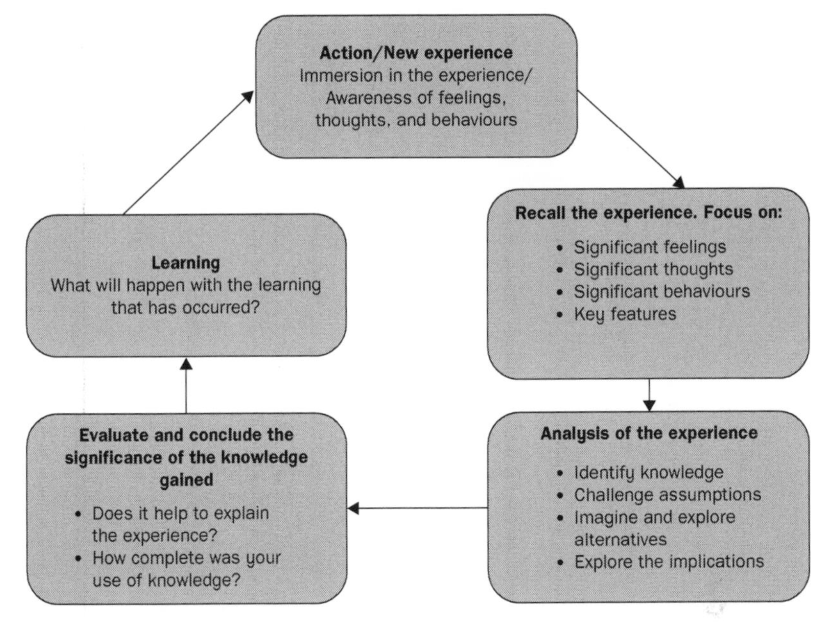


**Figure 7.5** Atkins and Murphy's framework for reflection
Source: Adapted from Atkins and Murphy (1994).

In Atkins and Murphy's framework, the stages are similar to those of Gibbs and therefore not too dissimilar from those of Borton or Rolfe. Apart from Johns' framework, which we discussed in detail in Chapter 5, frameworks such as those discussed here are fairly similar in nature and structure. Therefore, when choosing a reflective framework to use, as long as you underpin its use with the knowledge you now have of reflection, your understanding of the extended description detailed in Chapter 1, and the ten essential ingredients for successful reflection, you will be able to use the framework appropriately and with understanding, and gain a depth of reflection that is required to enhance your self-awareness and emotional intelligence.

## Thoughts and feelings

Let's now take a closer look at something all reflective frameworks ask us to address: our thoughts and feelings. In my experience, students are often unclear as to the difference between a thought and a feeling. However, this is important if we are really going to understand ourselves.

Have a go at the following exercise.

## Exercise 7.2: Thoughts or feelings?

Read the following statements. Put an **F** next to what you think is a feeling and a **T** next to what you think is a thought.

| | |
|---|---|
| I feel like that decision was unjust. | No one likes me. |
| I feel like I should have said something. | He shouldn't treat me that way. |
| I feel like there's a better way of doing this. | The future holds nothing for me. |
| I am afraid at night. | I don't want to be apprehensive about going into hospital. |
| I think I am really anxious about tomorrow. | I dread her birthday. |
| I'm missing the closeness I used to have with my mum. | I'm not good enough. |
| I am just really, really sad. | I feel really guilty about what I said. |
| | I am useless. |
| | I am worthless. |
| | I am depressed. |

Try to justify to yourself why you gave some statements an **F** and the others a **T**. Now compare your choices with my own below.

## Exercise 7.2 (continued)

| | |
|---|---|
| I feel like that decision was unjust. **T** | No one likes me. **T** |
| I feel like I should have said something. **T** | He shouldn't treat me that way. **T** |
| I feel like there's a better way of doing this. **T** | The future holds nothing for me. **T** |
| I am afraid at night. **F** | I don't want to be apprehensive about going into hospital. **T/F** |
| I think I am really anxious about tomorrow. **F** | I dread her birthday. **F** |
| I'm missing the closeness I used to have with my mum. **T** | I'm not good enough. **T** |
| I am just really, really sad. **F** | I feel really guilty about what I said. **F** |
| | I am useless. **T** |
| | I am worthless. **F** |
| | I am depressed. **T/F** |

On how many did we agree? Note that I gave some statements both an **F** and a **T** – both a thought and a feeling. This is because until each statement is discussed and unpicked, it might be deemed a thought or a feeling.

The purpose of this exercise has been to highlight that acknowledging what thoughts we are having and to distinguish those from feelings is not an easy task but is something we need to be able to do when reflecting if we are to really understand ourselves.

It is common when reflecting to say, 'I feel like I should have said something'. But this is in fact a thought and the feelings generated from this may include frustration, anger, and anxiety. You may say 'I think I am really anxious about tomorrow', but this is in fact a feeling you are having about tomorrow and it may be based upon the thought, 'I don't want to do my presentation in front of the whole class tomorrow'. So, in the reflective process and in using a framework to support us in our endeavour to reflect, understanding what a thought is and being able to differentiate thoughts from feelings are what will enable appropriate analysis to generate self-awareness.

Have a go at the final exercise in this chapter.

### Exercise 7.3: Using a framework

Consider the frameworks mentioned in this chapter, as well as that that of Johns in Chapter 5. Now choose an experience to reflect upon. Your task here is to have a go at using a framework to support your reflection and to evaluate this framework in light of what you now know.

Once you have chosen your framework and reflected, ask yourself the following questions:

- Did you find the chosen framework useful?
- Was it easy to use?
- If you had any difficulties, what were they?
- Did it allow you to reflect analytically?
- Do you feel you gained depth of understanding?
- Did it allow you to view your experience from the perspective of others?
- Did it allow you to challenge your thoughts, feelings, behaviour, and assumptions?
- Were you able to draw conclusions?
- Did it support you in learning from the experience?
- Did it help you to consider new action and then take action?

- Were you comfortable using this framework?
- Were you able to underpin it with the ten essential ingredients?
- Would you recommend it to a friend?
- Would you use it again?
- Now return to the first exercise in this chapter and compare what you have said here to your original evaluation of reflective frameworks. Do you now think differently?

Now let's consider what we have learned about reflective frameworks in this chapter. There are many more reflective models besides the five we have referred to here and in Chapter 1. These are discussed in the literature and the right one for you is the one you are most comfortable using and which helps you to generate the most understanding. We now know these frameworks can be a useful mechanism to support the reflective process. But we also know that these frameworks are only useful if you understand what the point and purpose of reflection are. In discussing these different frameworks, we saw that most are cyclical in nature and we can move between the stages quite fluidly. We learned that our extended description of reflection – given in full in Chapter 1 – and our ten essential ingredients underpin and enable the appropriate use of reflective cycles. With the knowledge you now have, based on your reading of the previous chapters, you could use one or more of these frameworks in combination, or even develop your own reflective framework that is bespoke for you. Reflective frameworks are there to support and help you and there is no single way of using them.

**Key points that can be taken from this chapter are:**

- There is more than one reflective framework for you to use, and the one you choose, if you decide to use one, must be the one you are most comfortable with.
- Any framework needs to be underpinned with the extended description of reflection and the ten essential ingredients for successful reflection.

- Kolb developed a learning cycle that is not a traditional reflective cycle, but incorporates reflection as a learning element.
- Reflective frameworks are not necessarily reflective *assignment* structures, but they can be used as frameworks within which to reflect in the written mode.
- We need to understand the difference between thoughts and feelings.

CHAPTER

# Reflective writing

## Learning outcomes

By the end of this chapter, you will be able to:

- Understand the concept of reflective writing
- Know the difference between reflective writing for your own benefit and writing for academic purposes
- Recognize that reflective writing for academic purposes is underpinned by all of the principles of normal academic discursive writing
- Know what the principles of academic writing are
- Know how to apply the principles of academic writing to reflective writing
- Utilize the reflective writing model discussed in this chapter
- Be confident in your ability to write reflectively.

We now can confidently say we know what reflection is. We have learned most of what we need to know about reflection and reflective practice in the previous chapters, including reflective frameworks and how to use them. What we have not yet touched upon is reflective writing for personal use and reflective writing for academic purposes, and this chapter will highlight the differences between the two.

## Reflective writing for personal, academic, and professional purposes

Reflective writing for personal use is everything that we have discussed in all of the previous chapters, but instead of talking about our experience with a critical friend or quietly contemplating by ourselves, we write our reflections down. We reflect by writing. When we reflect by writing for our own personal benefit, we may not necessarily abide by all of the academic rules of writing. We may not pay particular attention to our grammar, sentence construction, our use of paragraphs or spelling. This is not to say we don't use the literature to help underpin our knowledge with evidence, or to fill gaps in our knowledge, nor is it to say we don't reflect deeply, analytically, and critically on our experiences. We may just be that bit more relaxed about how we write when we reflect for ourselves in the written format. Indeed, when we write for ourselves it could be that no one else sees what we have written. But we still need to learn from our written reflections and our personal reflective writing still needs to be underpinned by the ten essential ingredients for successful reflection and our understanding of what reflection is.

Reflective writing for academic purposes is quite different. You will have been required to undertake at least one assessment for which you had to write a reflective essay. For example, at the university at which I teach our pre-registration nursing programme requires our students to write a reflective essay as their first piece of work to be assessed, in which they are asked to reflect on their experience of attending a module on professional values. They are expected to achieve a high standard of academic writing but also to demonstrate their skills in reflection. Not an easy feat for a first-year student nurse! Writing reflectively for academic purposes can be hard, as you are expected to combine academic writing with the added element of reflection, including all ten ingredients for successful reflection.

Reflective writing is now also a requirement of the Nursing and Midwifery Council's new revalidation process. Once you qualify, you will be required to write five accounts of times you have reflected. It is thus a professional requirement to be able to write about your own reflections. This shows how important it is to get to grips with reflective writing.

This chapter will take you through a process that will provide you with the understanding and tools you need when writing reflectively for personal use, for academic purposes and, in the case of NMC revalidation, for professional purposes.

I teach reflection and reflective writing across many different programmes and for students who are at different stages of their training. Whether the students I am teaching are pre-registration nurses or post-registration nurses returning to top up their diploma to a degree or starting their masters journey, one thing I have found extremely useful is recapping the principles of academic writing before they start to write reflectively. Remember that reflective writing (especially for the purpose of meeting an assignment brief) must at all times be underpinned by the principles of normal academic writing. The first part of this chapter will be dedicated to discussing the principles of academic writing. The latter part will be dedicated to a tool devised by Gillie Bolton for reflective writing that I think you may find very useful. If you use the two together, you should find you are able to write reflectively for any purpose.

But let us first concentrate on understanding the principles of academic writing.

## The principles of academic writing

Have a go at the following exercise.

### Exercise 8.1: The principles of academic writing

Imagine you are a qualified nurse and you are mentoring a student, who asks you, 'What makes a good academic piece of writing?'. Consider your own past experiences of writing and the feedback you received, then in the space below jot down what you think makes a good piece of academic writing.

A good piece of academic writing must have the following qualities:

Now compare what you have written with my own suggestions below. Do the two lists match?

**Exercise 8.1 (continued)**

A good piece of academic writing must have the following qualities:

- answers the question;
- contains material that is relevant to the question;
- has a logical macro-structure;
- has a solid introduction;
- has a fluid micro-structure;
- contains material that is accurate;
- makes appropriate use of literature;
- is critically analytical;
- makes appropriate use of language;
- is grammatically correct.

Having taught in a university setting for more than 14 years, and specifically having taught academic skills at degree, masters, and doctoral level, I have benefited from the expertise and advice of my colleagues and tried to answer the queries of my students during this time. I have distilled this experience into some core criteria for academic writing. The following are what I perceive to be the fundamental principles of academic writing. Let's look at each of these in turn, some of which warrant more discussion than others.

### *Answers the question*

Have you ever written an essay for which you received the following feedback: 'You need to adhere more closely to the assignment brief'? Or in the annotations at the side of your work there may have been a question mark, or a suggestion that you included irrelevant material. In a piece of academic writing, it is of absolute importance that you write about what the brief asks you to write about. In order to adhere to this principle, ensure as part of your planning that you do actually understand the brief. I had a student who once wrote me an amazing essay on cognitive behavioural therapy. Unfortunately, the student failed as the brief was to analyse the person-centred approach to counselling as it applies to nursing practice. In an academic piece of reflective work, you will be given an assignment brief and that brief will no doubt require you to reflect on something very particular. The trick here is to make sure you reflect on what the brief requires you to reflect on, not what you perceive to be important.

As for writing reflectively for your own personal benefit, by all means feel free to go wherever your reflection takes you.

### *Contains material that is relevant to the question*

This is similar to the previous principle in that if you understand the assignment brief, you should be able to ensure you only use material in your writing that meets the assignment brief. A trick of mine whenever I have written a paragraph is to . . . stop, breathe, and think. Then I ask myself:

'Does this relate to what I said I would discuss in my introduction?'

If the answer is *no*, then ask yourself:

'Can I make it relate?'

If the answer is *no* again, then remove the irrelevant information. If the answer is *yes*, then introduce a connecting sentence. You can use whatever material you want, as long as it relates to the framework for discussion provided in your introduction, justifying why you have included the material in your writing. What is it doing there, how does it support your points or arguments, does it relate to the brief?

This is a very useful tip in reflective writing, since it is easy to be consumed by your own thoughts and feelings that everything feels important (as it should), making it easy to go off at a tangent.

### *Has a logical macro-structure*

Now there is a certain amount of common sense to this principle, since I would guess that you all know what the structure of an essay is: introduction, middle, conclusion. This format provides a structure that supports the fluidity and logicality of our discussions. Now let me ask you, which out of the introduction, the middle, and the conclusion do you think is the most important?

My students normally offer up 'middle', as this is the main part of the discussion, or 'conclusion', as this is the part that pulls everything together and helps make sense of the discussion. However, I would suggest that it is the introduction that is the most important part of any academic piece of work. Take a look at Table 8.1, which will show you why.

**Table 8.1** The importance of the introduction

| Introduction and . . . | why it's so important |
|---|---|
| First impressions count | The introduction is what captures the reader's imagination. It makes us want to read more. If the introduction reads poorly, it usually impacts upon the quality of the rest of the discussion |
| It provides a framework for the discussion | The introduction lays down what it is you will be discussing in the main body of the text. This acts as your framework, your structure that stops you from going off at a tangent in your discussion. The introduction is what you use to check the relevance of your material against |
| It provides a rationale for your discussion | The introduction, if written well, will provide a rationale for your discussion. It will set the context of the discussion for the reader, so that the reader can immediately understand the point of the discussion and follow it |

It is also my experience that the introduction is often the most poorly written part of a student's piece of work. My healthcare students understand the importance of exercise, so I ask them, 'when going for a jog or run, what is the most difficult part?' The usual answer is . . . the first ten minutes. In these ten minutes, we try to find our pace, we try to match our breathing to our pace, and we try to run through the pain. After ten minutes, we have usually found our rhythm and could run for miles. This is the same as essay writing. Once we are into the main body, we ought to have found our rhythm and may even start to enjoy the writing. My advice here is to write your introduction, *and then rewrite it at the end*, so that its quality matches the rest of your essay.

The middle section is where we analyse and discuss the topic at hand, and the conclusion is where we draw together the main points we have made. The conclusion is very important in reflective writing, as this is where we pull together the learning that has taken place through the reflective writing. This is where we consider the action we will take and turn our reflection into reflective practice.

### *Has a solid introduction*

We have already discussed the importance of the introduction, but in highlighting its importance we also need to understand it needs to be solid and robust. There is no single way of writing an introduction. You may have been given quite prescriptive advice by your programme leaders who, in trying to be helpful, told you what to put in your introduction, how many words long it should be, or even that you didn't really need one!

However, the content and length of an introduction are totally dependent upon the essay question or brief you have been given. You can start an introduction with purpose, for instance:

> It is the purpose of the following reflective discussion to . . .
> The following reflective discussion will . . .
> It is the aim of the following discussion to critically reflect upon . . .

Or, you can start with some content from the first part of the main body, for example:

> Empathy has been described in the literature as the essential ingredient of the therapeutic relationship, as it enables the practitioner to accurately understand the internal frame of reference of the person in need of help. It is therefore the intention of the following reflective discussion to . . .

I would strongly advise that you write your introduction in a manner that you are comfortable with and that it provides a solid foundation for the rest of your essay.

### *Has a fluid micro-structure*

I imagine that not all of you know what we mean here by micro-structure. This is the telling of your story through the use of paragraphs. We use paragraphs to form the subset of a topic, or as the natural start to a new topic. But if we don't connect our paragraphs, the reader will become confused and won't be able to follow how we got from A to B. We must always remember that the reader is not in *our* head when we write, so we must make our transitions from one paragraph to another very clear using simple sentences, for example:

> Having fully understood what really prompted me to behave in the manner I did, I really needed to try and understand how I felt and how I impacted on those around me . . .

Clear transition phrases and clear links between paragraphs will take the reader on a journey that makes sense. Read a children's novel and you will notice that simple yet clever writing keeps a child on track with the storyline, even when they put the book down and pick it up again a week later.

### *Contains material that is accurate*

This principle is quite straightforward: think very carefully about the material you put in and the way you use the literature. As a module leader, I have read many reflective pieces written by qualified nurses working in the field of addiction. As experienced practitioners, they believe they have knowledge, but have written from intuition and at times ignorance instead of evidence, and their information has been inaccurate. An example of this is when a student wrote, 'All drug users are violent. . . '. This is actually not the case, and there is no evidence to suggest otherwise. Now if in the student's experience all drug users encountered have been violent, then it needs to be made explicit that this is the student's experience, and should not be generalized.

### *Makes appropriate use of the literature*

This is an important principle and one that is often misunderstood in relation to reflective writing. It is also an area where well-intentioned advice offered by lecturers to their students may not always be that helpful.

There are two elements to appropriate use of the literature. The first element relates to the way we acknowledge our sources of information and where we have gained our knowledge from in order to write our discussion. This ensures we are not passing off another person's work/ideas as our own. This is also about giving recognition to published authors. Within the university at which I work, we only use the Harvard referencing system; other universities may use a different system, say the Vancouver system. It is imperative that you know which system your university uses and that you seek support, attend workshops, and gain advice on how to apply the chosen system. Not using the correct system can have a negative impact on the marks you receive for your assignment and not using a system at all could lead to you being referred to a plagiarism committee.

The second element is the aspect that I would like us to focus our attention on, which is how we use the literature in order to create that academic discussion/debate. You will be told throughout your training that as nurses and healthcare practitioners, you need to be evidence-based in your practice. This means underpinning the care you provide with relevant, up-to-date evidence, literature, and other sources of information. This will help you to ensure you are practising safely, in accordance with the most up-to-date evidence, and that you are not simply basing your care on assumptions or personal opinions that may not be accurate.

The purpose of using the literature as it relates to our academic writing is to:

- create discussion;
- develop discussion;
- create debate;
- expand on points we have made;
- offer alternative viewpoints;
- enable things to be viewed from a different perspective;
- demonstrate we have engaged with the evidence and the literature that is out there;
- demonstrate that we can understand what we are reading;

- provide credibility to discussions we wish to develop;
- demonstrate we can understand the different types of evidence and how they should be used appropriately.

In relation to reflective writing (and this is where there often appears to be a lack of understanding), *all of the above apply*. Just because reflective writing is about you and your experience does not make it any less academic and any less in need of supporting references to relevant literature. So, all of the above apply – and then we can add the following:

- provide an evidence-based framework within which we can view and assess the knowledge we thought we had against the knowledge we should have;
- challenge our assumptions and judgements;
- enable us to fill the gaps in our knowledge that we identified in the reflective process;
- provide credibility to our own opinions on what we have experienced;
- enhance our understanding of our experience.

*Scenario 8.1*

Take a look at the following excerpt from a reflective piece of writing where the female student has made a reasonable attempt at using the literature, in amongst her reflection:

> Empathy is one of the most important components in therapeutic work, understanding an individual's feelings and situation, through their own perspective. Historically, professional support for Mary had been variable and sometimes threatening. I gave her an atmosphere of acceptance, important in inviting change (Miller and Rollnick 2002). I did not assume to give advice, encouraging her openly to discuss her drug use as valued by Miller (2010). Additionally, Norton (2011) suggests that therapeutic empathy mitigates anxiety and can regulate emotion, particularly with those who use drugs. However, I had got lost in Mary's world, losing the sense of 'as if' it were my world (Rogers 1980), it became my own, as if I was living it with my daughter again.

Can you see how this writer has attempted to use the literature to enhance the understanding she has gained from her experience and as a result enhance her reflective writing? You can now see how important appropriate use of the literature is as an academic principle.

Now, I would like you to consider how many references to use in your academic work. You may have been give advice similar to the following:

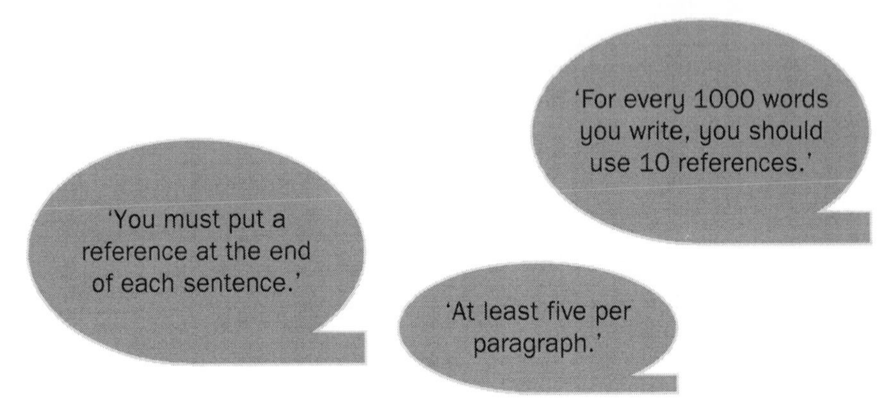


What is happening here is an attempt by lecturers to help students who are looking for 'concrete' numbers in relation to the amount of reading they need to do and ultimately the number of references they need to cite. When students ask my advice, instead of giving them a number I revert back to the points above on the purpose of using the literature in academic writing. I also tell them to read the question carefully and then apply thoughtfulness or common sense to the reading appropriate for the essay question or brief.

If you are asked to reflect on communication in nursing, there is an abundance of written material on the subject. If you are applying thoughtfulness, if you only cite two or three references, then this might suggest you have not read extensively around the subject matter. Remember you are trying to show you have engaged in research. If in doubt, refer back to the bullet points above and ask yourself: 'Have I used the literature in line with these points?'

### *Is critically analytical*

Also absolutely fundamental to academic writing is critical analysis. In Chapter 2, we discussed this principle in great detail, as it is also part of one of the ten essential ingredients for successful reflection. So we already know how important it is to reflection and reflective practice. What we discussed in Chapter 2 applies equally to academic and reflective writing.

Revisit Chapter 2 and remind yourself of what critical analysis is, as being critically analytical and applying what we learned in that chapter to our writing ensures that we are not just scratching the surface of our discussion or debate. It ensures we are penetrating the discussion to a meaningful level and it prevents us from writing descriptively.

### *Makes appropriate use of language and good grammar*

I will discuss these two principles together because I feel they go hand in hand. At degree level, we do expect grammatical correctness and use of appropriate language in written work. This however is not always that simple. I remember sitting my Viva for my doctorate and the very experienced external examiner stated that I had no idea how to use a comma, and 'did I expect her not to breathe when reading my work?'. I can laugh about this now, but at the time she was right. Grammar for me has never been easy, and it may not be for you. This is okay and is something that you can perfect with practice and by allowing others to view your work and to give you advice.

In relation to language, my advice is not to use complicated language or words if you do not understand their meaning because this will show through, as you may use them out of context. There is nothing wrong with using simple language to discuss complex terms. What you need to avoid is colloquial language. This is a type of language that is perceived as informal and might include slang usually related to local dialect. In academic writing, you need to be mindful of the terms you use, of the way in which you construct sentences, and of the professionalism that needs to be evident. Because of the nature of reflective writing, it is very easy to revert to a chatty, colloquial style of writing. Be aware of this and be conscious of how you express yourself.

If you are like me and you find a word you like and become comfortable with, you may find yourself over-using it so that it becomes repetitive. The answer is to use a thesaurus to provide you with other words that have a similar meaning. Add to your vocabulary. I guarantee by the time you have finished your nurse training you will speak and talk quite differently to the way you do now. During your time as a student nurse, you will converse with patients, carers, other nurses, senior managers, doctors, and consultants. All of these conversations will expand your vocabulary. Take on board these experiences and grow and develop both your vocabulary and articulation.

We have now covered the basic and essential principles of academic writing that also underpin reflective writing (you may well uncover more as you become more practised, or devise your own). Whether writing reflectively for your own personal benefit or to meet academic requirements, take a look at the following framework that will help you in your endeavours.

## Through the mirror writing

Gillie Bolton has written extensively on reflection and has focused her endeavours on teaching us how to write reflectively. She is an author who has demonstrated passion not just for reflection but reflection through writing. We have met Gillie Bolton in previous chapters and her main method of reflecting and being reflexive is what she calls 'through the mirror writing' (Bolton 2010). She refers to through the mirror writing as 'trusting the authority of the writing hand' (Bolton 2010: 104), letting the mind connect with the hand and letting the ideas flow.

In her book *Reflective Practice: Writing and Professional Development*, which I highly recommend, you will learn a great deal on how to write reflectively. Bolton dedicates a whole chapter to the 'how' of reflection and reflexivity, where she describes in detail how to undertake through the mirror writing. This type of writing sees the content of our writing as its foundation – not grammar, language or other rules. The authors of reflective writing are their own first readers whereby no one else will read their work without expressed permission. When writing in this manner, Bolton (2010) is clear that people need to rid themselves of the sense that teachers or editors are ready to correct and control content. The author has full authority over his or her own writing and there is no wrong way, allowing for almost anything to be written uncensored. This type of writing (writing reflectively solely for personal use) remains with as a draft and does not need to be readied for assessment or publication. Bolton tells us her method is about the process not the product, a discussion we have had previously about reflection in general. Bolton (2010) suggests that her method of reflecting is exploratory and expressive, undertaken often at speed; it is a dynamic, initially private process of discovery.

To achieve through the mirror writing, a way of reflecting deeply and analytically through the written word, we need to proceed through six stages. These six stages teach us to free write and write reflectively – that is, connect mind to hand and just let the content flow with no thought for anything else other than what we want to say on paper. Box 8.1 provides an explanation of each of the six stages.

## Box 8.1: Through the mirror writing

| *Stages* | *Explanation* |
| --- | --- |
| **Stage 1** | Preparation for free writing. This stage gives us permission to write freely. At this point, we consider a topic – it could be anything. It could be about a pet, family, work, etc. We then make ourselves comfortable and allocate ourselves a brief amount of time to write about whatever we want – letting our mind connect to our hand as we write without any constraints. |
| **Stage 2** | We now free write about the experience we wish to reflect upon. This can take as long as we wish. Again we do not concern ourselves with worrying about grammar, spelling, punctuation or phrasing. We just write about the topic. |
| **Stage 3** | This is where we take time to read the free writing, digesting the story we have written. We read and ask questions – but not only do we ask questions, we also answer the questions making notes as we go. We hold a Socratic dialogue with ourselves. We become our own critical friend. We are person-centred with ourselves. |
| **Stage 4** | At this point, we find a person we can trust. We ask them to read our free writing, to read the questions we asked and the answers we provided. We ask them to act as our external critical friend, and to ask further questions of our writing that we then try to answer. This is called the 'reflective conversation'. |

**Stage 5** We now do what we have discussed in previous chapters – we become reflexive by writing about the same experience but from a different point of view. We write about our experience from the point of view of another person who was part of the experience. This allows us to see how our experience impacted on those around us, and provides us with a different perspective.

**Stage 6** It is at this stage, when we have reflected quite deeply, we can – if we so choose, or if there is a requirement of us to do so – prepare our reflective writing for academic purposes, going through the content and formatting, shaping, and reworking the information into a piece that is suitable for academic purposes.

Source: Adapted from Bolton (2010).

What we have here is a very useful framework that can support the development of our reflective writing. Bolton's method of reflective writing can be of benefit in developing reflective skills and confidence in becoming reflexive when reflecting 'on action' in the written format. It can help us to develop the skills required so that we can tackle academic reflective assignments with confidence. However, we need to acknowledge that this method requires time and effort on our behalf and is not a quick undertaking. This type of reflection will also depend heavily upon the critical friend's involvement at stage 4, if at stage 3 we are not comfortable or confident with knowing what questions to ask of our own reflection. Hopefully, previous chapters will help you with this stage, especially our discussion of Johns' and Rolfe's frameworks where we are provided with Socratic questions.

Have a go at the following:

## Exercise 8.2: Reflective writing: the through the mirror method

Consider an experience you wish to reflect on and take learning from. Follow Gillie Bolton's six stages of through the mirror writing.

Consider the process of reflective writing in this manner, then evaluate your experience of it.

- How did you find the process?
- Did you go through all the stages?
- Which stage did you find most useful?
- Which stage did you find most difficult to complete?
- Do you think it has helped you to start to get to grips with reflective writing?
- Do you feel you learned anything from undertaking reflective writing in his manner?

This chapter has taught us about the principles that underpin academic writing. We have further learned that that these principles underpin our reflective writing, both when writing for personal benefit and when writing for academic purposes. We have been shown a useful tool, the six stages of *through the mirror writing* that will provide us with a framework within which we can develop our reflective writing skills and ensure that a deep level of analysis is achieved.

**Key points that can be taken from this chapter are:**

- There are a number of principles that underpin academic writing.
- These principles can be learned, practised, and perfected over time.
- These principles also underpin our reflective writing.
- We can write reflectively for personal benefit and for academic purposes.
- Reflective writing can be no less academic than our normal discursive essays.
- Using a framework such as through the mirror writing can help us develop our ability to reflect in the written format.
- Giving ourselves permission to free write can develop our ability to truly acknowledge how we feel and allow us to ask questions that take our writing to a deeper analytical level.

CHAPTER

# Final thoughts and recommendations

> Two fundamental skills necessary for all healthcare professionals are firstly, to discover and reflect on their own voice and secondly to enable others to hear and claim their own.
>
> (Ghaye and Lillyman 2000: 55)

We have throughout this book discovered our voice: our reflective voice.

## Learning outcomes

By the end of this chapter, you will be able to:

- Review your knowledge of reflection and reflective practice
- Review how the ten essential ingredients support the reflective process
- Understand how transformational learning and reflection are related and support each other
- Review and recollect the questions we need to ask ourselves in the reflective process
- Reflect on whether we have any gaps in our knowledge relating to this subject matter.

In Chapter 1, we became familiar and comfortable with the notion of reflection, what it is and its purpose. We discovered the new extended description of reflection, which reveals reflection as a natural, transparent, developmental process that is a diverse journey of self-discovery rather than a static, prescriptive, ritualistic reflection on the mechanics of practice. The extended description tells us that reflection is more than a one-dimensional concept – we have found it to be a concept that is process-orientated and that enables enhancement of self-awareness, learning in relation to our impact on others, while supporting understanding of the external environment and the influence it can have on our behaviour, thoughts, and feelings. We have found that reflection can enhance our emotional intelligence and allow us to create and discover new knowledge.

Sometimes, the literature on reflection characterizes the process as static, broad, and related to one of two concepts of reflecting: 'reflecting in-action' or 'reflecting on-action'. The extended description of reflection is the result of giving staff and students a voice in order to understand their experiences of learning and teaching reflection, and it offers a more diverse, individualistic way of viewing reflection and reflective practice. This description offers a non-static view of reflection, allowing for reflection to be about the person reflecting, fluidly; it is not prescriptive and acknowledges the free ideas associated with reflecting. It does not say we can only reflect in or on action, but that we can reflect pre-action or mindfully all the time. The extended description does not perceive reflection as task-orientated or outcome-generated, and I feel it is more useful to student nurses and others engaged in reflective practice as it is not time-oriented or limited to particular incidents, but promotes lifelong learning.

Reflection and reflective practice are also important for personal development in terms of gaining self-awareness and enhancing emotional intelligence. They are also important for professional development in relation to our clinical practice.

In Chapter 1, I suggested that after reading the chapters in this book, we revisit the extended description of reflection printed there. So here it is again:

**A new, extended description of reflection**

'Reflection is an essential, engaging process that allows the reflector to frame and reframe their reality that is being experienced moment by moment. It requires us to utilize skills of communication, to become our own person-centred therapists, understanding ourselves in relation to experiences we are about to have, are having or have had, empathically and with accuracy, then stepping beyond the self and using this knowledge gained to understand how we may then have impacted on those around us. For this process to bear fruit, we must leave arrogance and complacency at the door, be kind and compassionate, offering ourselves unconditional positive regard, be actively engaged in mindfulness, consciously aware of the self in the moment, open to learning and sourcing new knowledge if the knowledge is not already known to us, using the new knowledge gained to develop ourselves personally and professionally in a critically analytical manner. When fully engaged in the reflective process, the experience can be humbling as we realize we are not perhaps what we assumed ourselves to be, yet also rewarding as we confirm that our best may have at that time been good enough.'

Now, is there anything about this description you still don't understand? Are there any elements that we have not covered, discussed, and learned about in the previous chapters? Revisit the notes you made in Chapter 1 when you first read the extended description. Do you think you understand the description well enough to address any questions you had then?

In Chapters 5 and 7, you were introduced to some frameworks of reflection and reflective practice. These frameworks can be presented in the form of reflective cycles, reflective models, dialogues or models of writing. However, we now know that to reflect successfully we need to understand reflection, we need to have the right attitude, and we need a combination of skills. Few frameworks appear to take all of this into account and as well as teach us how to reflect, provide us with the skills to do so. Therefore, the extended description and the new unique approach to reflection – the ten essential ingredients, devised following research into the teaching and learning experiences of students and staff in relation to reflection, and listening to the voices of the research participants – offers us a new way of reflecting that takes into account the attitude and skills required and our own individuality by not prescribing *how to*. It communicates to the reflector what is needed for effective reflection and allows the reflector to review their attitude and skills in light of these requirements while highlighting our own unique areas for development.

Let us look again at the ten essential ingredients for successful reflection and, unlike in Chapter 1 where we first met them, look at them alongside their unique narrative. The ingredients are addressed in the same order as they appeared in Chapters 2–6.

**The ten essential ingredients for successful reflection**

| | |
|---|---|
| **Academic skills** | 'Reflecting is not a vivid description of an event, a situation or an experience, but a review of the experience prior to, during or after, in a critically analytical manner. This critical analysis must be supported by knowledge, particularly knowledge that can bridge the theory–practice gap and so be meaningful to practice experience. New knowledge gained is then amalgamated with the old and current knowledge, from which the person can then synthesize a new way of being, or expand and enhance the current way of being.' |
| **Knowledge** | 'The practitioner, in order to evaluate and reflect upon what they are experiencing in the clinical setting, needs to have a level of knowledge that they can refer to and evaluate their experience against. If they do not have the existing knowledge, they need to know how to source the knowledge so that they may bridge that theory–practice gap, and enhance their ability to understand the experience they are reflecting on, prior to, in action or on action.' |
| **Attitudinal qualities** | 'The driving force of successful engagement with the reflective process. The practitioner needs to be humble to the process, be open, honest, and willing, having the motivation to understand and learn. The practitioner needs to be brave, courageous, and confident in order to encourage the honesty required in the process. Kindness, compassion, and offering unconditional positive regard to oneself enable openness.' |

| | |
|---|---|
| **Self-awareness** | 'The practitioner needs to have a current level of awareness of self, a perception of how they perceive themselves to be. It is this current knowledge of self that is the basis for the reflective process. Self-awareness allows the individual to be honest about how they perceive themselves to 'be' in the experience. It is this existing knowledge of the self that is also agreed, challenged, developed, and overturned, in and by, the reflective process.' |
| **Being person-centred** | 'The reflector has vast resources for self-understanding. These resources for self-understanding can be accessed if we are person-centred with ourselves. Recognizing we have our own unique subjective view of the world (our individual phenomenology) allows us to create a climate whereby we can get to know ourselves and gain a deeper understanding of ourselves in relation to our experiences. With understanding, a heightened level of self-awareness grows. We are able to develop both personally and professionally.' |
| **Being empathic** | 'The practitioner needs to want to understand themselves in relation to their experiences accurately. They need to use the skills of empathic questioning and responding to allow for deeper analysis of their thoughts, feelings, and behaviour in relation to what they are reflecting on. Not only this, they need to also be able to use their empathy to understand how others perceive them and the experience.' |
| **Communication** | 'The practitioner needs to be able to articulate themselves in a verbal and non-verbal manner, whether this is to themselves or to another person. They need to have the communication skills that allow them to act as their own internal supervisor. These communication skills include the skills of Socratic questioning and empathic responding.' |
| **Mindfulness** | 'The practitioner needs to be cognisant of themselves, their surroundings, their behaviour, thoughts, and feelings. An acute awareness of the experience they are having or have had moment by moment and in the context of others.' |

| | |
|---|---|
| **Being process-orientated** | 'Reflection is not about the outcome/output, but about the process that takes place when reflecting. Reflection may not always be so smooth as to guarantee a definitive outcome. As much learning can take place from the process as can occur from the result.' |
| **Being strategic** | 'Reflecting is not a flippant, inconsequential recap of an event, but a deliberate, controlled, conscious consideration of an experience. The reflector must be cognisant that every decision they make as a result of reflection has a "ripple effect". The actions they take from the reflective process will not only impact upon the practitioner reflecting but on those around them.' |

Here we have our new unique approach to successful reflection, the ten essential ingredients: ingredients that establish the need for the person reflecting to adopt a certain way of thinking about themselves, to hold a certain attitude or mentality towards the reflective process, to frame themselves within a very particular paradigm (person-centred) within which they can safely and comfortably analyse and evaluate their experience, getting to know their genuine self. Ingredients that require the reflector to recognize the need to harness the intellectual, academic skills we use on a daily basis, putting into practice the knowledge we already have so that we can identify those areas where further research is required. Ingredients that empower the reflector to understand the value in the process, to recognize the learning that also takes place as we reflect – not only after the event.

Using these ingredients for reflection is akin to mixing the ingredients to make a cake. The blending together of these ingredients gives us the final product – a successful reflective practitioner.

We have viewed elements of the extended description at the end of each chapter to determine the location of each ingredient within the description. This allows us to see the connection between the description and the ingredients that support it, and provides us with the necessary elements in order to reflect.

Having worked our way through the chapters in this book, we know what reflection is and what we need to do and be to reflect successfully. We have also learned that reflective frameworks can be useful when we are starting out on our reflective journey. These frameworks provide a very useful structure to support us in our endeavours to reflect until it becomes second nature to us.

Have another look at the ten essential ingredients. Are there any you would like to add? Maybe you've come up with one or two of your own.

I have in this book focused my attention on the act of reflection and what we need to be and do to enable successful reflection. However, we need to be mindful of how we prepare ourselves to become effective reflective practitioners. Christopher Johns, a prolific writer on reflection and an absolute supporter of its benefits, encapsulated aspects of self within a framework of reflective practice that we can use to begin our engagement with the reflective process. Johns has composed a *way of being* that amalgamates different aspects of ourselves and our attitude into what he calls the 10 C's of reflection (Johns 2000: 36). Take a look at Box 9.1.

**Box 9.1: The 10 C's**

| | |
|---|---|
| **Commitment** | The motivation and commitment to getting to know yourself within your practice. |
| **Contradiction** | Recognizing, analysing, and understanding the difference between your actual practice and what it should be. |
| **Conflict** | Not shying away from conflict but recognizing it and using it to empower yourself to better your practice. |
| **Challenge and support** | Challenging your value base, confronting your norms, morals, and attitude in a manner that is about learning in a safe environment. |
| **Catharsis** | Recognizing any negative thoughts and feelings and understanding them, working though any issues that may arise that may impact on you and your practice. |

| | |
|---|---|
| **Creation** | Being reflexive. Identifying different perspectives. Moving beyond self to see and understand new ways of viewing and responding to practice. |
| **Connection** | Using the learning to enhance your current practice, but recognizing that experiences are transitional and come and go and develop over time. |
| **Caring** | Acknowledging that compassion and good practice are expected and a normal part of everyday practice. It should embody who you are. |
| **Congruence** | Reflection as a mirror for caring. The way you care for yourself and wish to understand yourself is the same as that applied to the care of a patient. |
| **Constructing personal knowledge in practice** | Weaving personal knowing with relevant extant theory in constructing knowledge. Recognizing what we already know, interweaving this with information from the evidence base. |

Source: Adapted from Johns (2000: 36).

Engaging with the 10 C's is about the reflector's attitude to learning before beginning reflecting as well as what needs to occur during the reflective process. Whereas the ten essential ingredients for successful reflection relate in the main to what occurs during the reflective process itself, the 10 C's offer facets of what we need to engage with and adopt as a *way of being*, before and whilst engaging with our ingredients in the reflective process. There is, however, an overlap between the two, as the 10 C's require the potential reflector to be open to learning about themselves, to be able to acknowledge what their attitudes and perceptions are, to be open to challenging their current ideologies, to have the ability to be empathic, to view the world as others may see it, and to be able to combine evidence-based theory with personal knowing in the construction of new knowledge. What we see in aspects of Johns' 10 C's, unlike other frameworks, is a fundamental *way of being* – or attitude towards reflection and learning before we even begin to reflect.

Having read this book I hope you now understand the importance and usefulness of reflection. This book has introduced the notion of transformational – or, as others call it, transformative – learning (reflectivity). The principal theme and power of transformational or transformative learning is a fundamental change in perspective that transforms the way we as adults understand and interact with our world. If we can understand how we interact with our world and then change that interaction if it no longer works for us, then the authority we have over the way we live our own lives and ultimately the way we experience our lives and the happiness that we can gain are immense. Reflection and reflective thinking is the principal means of supporting and fostering such transformations of perception and interaction.

More than 25 years ago, Mezirow grouped reflection under three headings. Rather than viewing reflection as in or on action, Mezirow (1991: 104) defined reflection as

> . . . [a] process of critically assessing the content, process, or premise(s) of our efforts to interpret and give meaning to an experience.

According to Mezirow (1991), *content reflection* is an examination of the content or description of a problem. *Process reflection* involves checking on the problem-solving strategies that are being used, and *premise reflection* leads the learner to a transformation of meaning perspectives. That is, we can alter the way we perceive our experiences and give new meaning to them, which in our extended description of reflection we call framing and re-framing. These three areas of reflection align well with our extended description, as it allows the reflector to reflect whenever and however they feel is most appropriate, but it accounts for the different contexts that underpin the process and purpose of or need for reflection. Mezirow is more explicit about the areas reflection can cover, whereas our extended description is more implicit and allows for individual interpretation.

We spoke previously about transformative learning and this is what Mezirow calls reflectivity. To view how reflection is situated within transformative learning and to provide further support to reflection being the crux of transformative or transformational learning,

Mezirow provides a tool that allows us to view the elements of transformative learning so we can see where reflection fits in. He called this 'reflectivity' and proposed that it has seven levels (see Box 9.2).

## Box 9.2: Mezirow's seven levels of reflectivity

| *Level* | *Description* |
|---|---|
| 1 | Reflectivity – awareness of a specific question. What is the specific thing we wish to reflect upon? |
| 2 | Affective reflectivity – awareness of how we feel about the way we are perceiving, thinking or acting/habits. Our thoughts/feelings/morals/values. |
| 3 | Discriminant reflectivity – assessment of the worth of our perceptions, thoughts, actions, habits, of doing things. Identifying the relationship we have to the situation we are reflecting upon. |
| 4 | Judgemental reflectivity – making judgements about the experience and being aware of our value judgements, perceptions, thoughts, actions, and habits within the experience. |
| 5 | Conceptual reflectivity – internal questioning of our values. |
| 6 | Psychic reflection – recognition of the habit of making judgements based on limited information. Recognizing that our personality can influence our perception of the experiences, our actions, and our thinking. |
| 7 | Theoretical reflection – awareness of the reasons for our habitual pre-conceived ideas and judgements. |

Source: Adapted from Mezirow (1981).

Mezirow's seven levels of reflectivity help us to understand that reflection has both affective (emotional) and cognitive (thought) domains. This further supports our extended description and ingredients, which acknowledge the need for affective and cognitive factors.

So let's now pull everything together that we have learned by reading this book. Have a go at the following exercise.

## Exercise 9.1: Pulling it all together

We now know what reflection is and we have our extended description. We also know the essential ingredients that make up the reflective process and we understand that the key to adult, transformational learning is the reflective conversation we have with ourselves or another person or persons. Have a go at answering the following questions:

- What do you now understand reflection to be?
- Do you think the ten essential ingredients are a necessary part of reflection?
- How would you use the ten essential ingredients?
- If you were to use a framework for reflection, which one would you use and why?
- What have you found most useful about this book?
- When do you think you will find reflection most helpful?
- How do you feel about reflection now?

Now write down some prompt questions to support you in the reflective process. Remember what you have learned as a result of working your way through this book. Reflection is about understanding ourselves within the experiences we have had, are having or are going to have, in order to learn and change if need be. What kinds of questions do you think will enable you to have that Socratic dialogue with yourself that will allow for deep analytical understanding? You can revisit Johns' and Rolfe's models to give you some ideas but try to come up with some of your own.

Finally, here are my recommendations based upon many years of engaging with reflection. Please feel free to add to or modify this list to suit your own needs.

**Recommendations for successful reflection**

- Accept reflection as a natural part of who you are.
- Embody the notion of reflection.
- Recognize the analytical nature of reflection.
- Acknowledge the value of reflection.

- Know that reflective writing is no less academic than your normal assignments.
- Practise reflecting as often as you can.
- Reflect in a manner that suits you.
- Ask your clinical mentors/personal tutors to offer you guided reflection.
- Don't just reflect on the negative experiences you have.
- Recognize the value in learning from the positive.
- Initiate a reflective practice group with your peers where you can reflect together.
- Practise using different frameworks in order to find the one that most suits you.
- Keep revisiting the extended description of reflection to ensure you always understand the point of what we are doing here.
- View reflection as process-orientated and acknowledge the learning that takes place as part of this process.
- Always combine the ten essential ingredients when reflecting, in whatever mode and manner you reflect.
- Remember always to put into practice the learning that occurs as a result of reflecting.

# A final word

> Here is Edward Bear, coming downstairs now, bump, bump, bump, on the back of his head, behind Christopher Robin. It is, as far as he knows, the only way of coming downstairs, but sometimes he feels that there really is another way, if only he could stop bumping for a moment and think of it.
>
> (Winnie the Pooh, in Milne 1973: 49)

We now have the tools to stop bumping and think! This book has provided us with the understanding and necessary skills to be able to stop, take stock, and reflect – to learn about ourselves, to understand our experiences and how they affect us, to know how we affect those around us, and how our external environment impacts upon us. We now have the tools to generate greater self-awareness.

Practice makes perfect. In practising and perfecting the art of reflection and reflective practice, you will become emotionally intelligent individuals and practitioners. You will be capable of understanding yourselves and how to use that understanding within the therapeutic relationships you have with those you care for, and in the relationships that shape your personal lives. You will understand the impact you have on others and be able to use that understanding to empathically *be* with another person.

I hope that you have enjoyed reading this book, and I hope that you have taken learning from it that is useful to you.

# References


Allport, G.W. (1935) Attitudes, in C. Murchison (ed.) *Handbook of Social Psychology*. Worcester, MA: Clark University Press.

Archer, M.S. (2007) *Making Our Own Way Through the World: Human reflexivity and social mobility*. Cambridge: Cambridge University Press.

Atkins, S. (2004) Developing underlying skills in the move towards reflective practice, in C. Bulman and S. Schutz (eds.) *Reflective Practice in Nursing*, 3rd edn. Oxford: Blackwell.

Atkins, S. and Murphy, C. (1993) Reflection: a review of the literature, *Journal of Advanced Nursing*, 18 (8): 1188–92.

Atkins, S. and Murphy, C. (1994) Reflective practice, *Nursing Standard*, 8 (39): 49–56.

Bandman, E.L. and Bandman, B. (1995) *Critical Thinking in Nursing*, 2nd edn. Norwalk, CT: Appleton & Lange.

Beckett, T. (1969) A candidate's reflections on the supervisory process, *Contemporary Psychoanalysis*, 5: 169–79.

Bolton, G. (2010) *Reflective Practice: Writing and professional development*, 3rd edn. London: Sage.

Bond, M. and Holland, S. (1998) *Skills of Clinical Supervision for Nurses*. Buckingham: Open University Press.

Borton, T. (1970) *Reach, Touch and Teach*. London: Hutchinson.

Boud, D., Keogh, R. and Walker, D. (1985) *Reflection: Turning experience into learning*. London: Kogan Page.

Boyd, E. and Fales, A. (1983) Reflective learning: key to learning from experience, *Journal of Humanistic Psychology*, 23 (2): 99–117.

Bozarth, J.D. (2002) Empirically supported treatment: epitome of the 'specificity myth', in J.C. Watson, R.N. Goldman and M.S. Warner (eds.) *Client-centered and Experiential Psychotherapy in the 21st Century: Advances in theory, research, and practice.* Ross-on-Wye: PCCS Books.

Brammer, L.M. and MacDonald, G. (1996) *The Helping Relationship: Process and skills*, 6th edn. London: Allyn & Bacon.

Casement, P. (1985) *On Learning from the Patient.* New York: Guilford Press.

Ciarrochi, J.V. and Bailey, A. (2008) *A CBT Practitioner's Guide to ACT: How to bridge the gap between cognitive behavioural therapy and acceptance and commitment therapy.* Oakland, CA: New Harbinger Publications.

Clarke, N.M. (2014) A person-centred enquiry into the teaching and learning experiences of reflection and reflective practice – part one, *Nurse Education Today*, 34 (9): 1219–24.

Cooke, M. and Matarasso, B. (2005) Promoting reflection in mental health nursing practice: a case illustration using problem-based learning, *International Journal of Mental Health Nursing*, 14 (4): 243–8.

Dalley, J. (2009) Purpose and value in reflection, in H. Bulpitt and M. Deane (eds.) *Connecting reflective learning teaching and assessment.* Occasional Paper #10. London: Higher Education Academy.

Dewey, J. (1933) *How We Think.* Boston, MA: D.C. Heath.

Dexter, G. and Wash, M. (2001) *Psychiatric Nursing Skills.* London: Thomas Nelson.

Driscoll, J. (2007) *Practising Clinical Supervision: A reflective approach for healthcare professionals*, 2nd edn. Oxford: Elsevier.

Eckroth-Bucher, M. (2010) Self-awareness: a review and analysis of a basic nursing concept, *Advances in Nursing Science*, 33 (4): 297–309.

Freshwater, D. (1998) The philosopher's stone, in C. Johns and D. Freshwater (eds.) *Transforming Nursing Through Reflective Practice.* Oxford: Blackwell.

Freshwater, D. (2000) *Transforming learning in nurse education.* PhD thesis, University of Nottingham, Nottingham.

Freshwater, D. (2007) Reflective practice and clinical supervision: two sides of the same coin?, in V. Bishop (ed.) *Clinical Supervision in Practice*, 2nd edn. Basingstoke: Palgrave Macmillan.

Ghaye, T. (ed.) (1996) *Reflection and Action for Healthcare Professionals: A reader.* Newcastle-upon-Tyne: Pentaxion Press.

Ghaye, T. and Lillyman, S. (eds.) (2000) *Effective Clinical Supervision: The role of reflection.* Dinton: Mark Allen Publishing.

Gibbs, G. (1988) *Learning by Doing: A guide to teaching and learning methods.* Oxford: Further Education Unit.

Hagland, M.R. (1998) Reflection: a reflex action?, *Intensive and Critical Care Nursing,* 14 (2): 96–100.

Heath, H. (1998) Keeping a reflective practice diary: a practical guide, *Nurse Education Today*, 18 (7): 592–8.

Hofstadter, D. (2007) *I Am a Strange Loop.* New York: Basic Books.

Jasper, M. (2003) *Foundations in Nursing Healthcare: Beginning reflective practice.* Andover: Cengage Learning.

Johns, C. (2000) *Becoming a Reflective Practitioner.* Oxford: Blackwell.

Johns, C. (2004) *Becoming a Reflective Practitioner*, 2nd edn. Oxford: Blackwell.

Johns, C. (2005) Expanding the gates of perception, in C. Johns and D. Freshwater (eds.) *Transforming Nursing Through Reflective Practice*, 2nd edn. Oxford: Blackwell.

Kirschenbaum, H. and Henderson, V.L. (eds.) (1989) *The Carl Rogers Reader.* London: Constable.

Kolb, D.A. (1984) *Experiential Learning.* Englewood Cliffs, NJ: Prentice-Hall.

Luft, J. and Ingham, H. (1955) *The Johari Window: A graphic model for interpersonal relations.* Los Angeles, CA: University of California Western Training Lab.

Mantzoukas, S. and Jasper, M.A. (2004) Reflective practice and daily ward reality: a covert power game, *Journal of Clinical Nursing*, 13: 925–33.

Mayer, R.E. (2002) *Teaching for Meaningful Learning to Occur.* Upper Saddle River, NJ: Prentice-Hall.

McCormack, B. and McCance, T.V. (2006) Development of a framework for person-centred nursing, *Journal of Advanced Nursing*, 56 (5): 472–9.

McCormack, B. and McCance, T. (2010) *Person-centred Nursing: Theory and practice.* Oxford: Wiley-Blackwell.

Mearns, D. and Thorne, B. (1988) *Person-centred Counselling in Action.* London: Sage.

Mezirow, J. (1981) A critical theory of adult learning and education, *Adult Education Quarterly*, 32 (1): 3–24.

Mezirow, J. (1991) *Transformative Dimensions of Adult Learning.* San Francisco, CA: Jossey-Bass.

Miller, G. (2010) *Learning the Language of Addiction Counselling*, 3rd edn. New York: Wiley.

Miller, W.R and Rollnick, S. (2002) *Motivational Interviewing: Preparing people for change.* New York: Guilford Press.

Milne, A.A. (1973) *Winnie the Pooh.* London: Egmont.

Moon, J. (2001) *Reflection in higher education learning.* PDP Working Paper #4. Exeter: LTSN Generic Centre.

Nelson-Jones, R. (2006) *Theory and Practice of Counselling and Therapy*. London: Sage.

Nicholl, H. and Higgins, A. (2004) Reflection in pre-registration nursing curricula, *Journal of Advanced Nursing*, 46 (6): 578–85.

Norton, L. (2011) Developing empathy: a case study exploring transference and counter-transference with adolescent females who self-injure, *Journal of Social Work Practice*, 25 (1): 95–107.

Nursing and Midwifery Council (NMC) (2015a) *The Code: Professional standards of practice and behaviour for nurses and midwives* [available at: https://www.nmc.org.uk/globalassets/sitedocuments/nmc-publications/nmc-code.pdf; accessed 17 July 2017].

Nursing and Midwifery Council (NMC) (2015b) *Standards for Competence for Registered Nurses* [available at: https://www.nmc.org.uk/globalassets/sitedocuments/standards/nmc-standards-for-competence-for-registered-nurses.pdf; accessed 13 December 2016].

Palmer, A.N., Burns, S. and Bulman, C. (eds.) (2000) *Reflective Practice in Nursing*. Oxford: Blackwell.

Paul R. (1993) *Critical Thinking: What every person needs to survive in a rapidly changing world*. Santa Rosa, CA: Foundation for Critical Thinking.

Pierson, W. (1998) Reflection and nurse education, *Journal of Advanced Nursing*, 27: 165–70.

Rogers, C.R. (1951) *Client-centered Therapy*. Boston, MA: Houghton Mifflin.

Rogers, C.R. (1957) The necessary and sufficient conditions of therapeutic personality change, *Journal of Consulting Psychology*, 21: 95–103.

Rogers, C.R. (1959) A theory of therapy, personality, and interpersonal relationships, as developed in the client-centered framework, in S. Koch (ed.) *Psychology: A study of a science, Vol. 3: Formulations of the person and the social context*. New York: McGraw-Hill.

Rogers, C.R. (1967) The interpersonal relationship in the facilitation of learning, in R. Leeper (ed.) *Humanizing Education*. Alexandria, VA: Association for Supervision and Curriculum Development.

Rogers, C.R. (1980) *A Way of Being*. Boston, MA: Houghton Mifflin.

Rogers, C.R. (1986) A client-centred/person-centred approach to therapy, in A. Kutash and A. Wolf (eds.) *Psychotherapist's Casebook*. San Francisco, CA: Jossey-Bass.

Rolfe, G. (2011) Models and frameworks for critical reflection, in G. Rolfe, M. Jasper and J. Freshwater (eds.) *Critical Reflection in Practice: Generating knowledge for care*, 2nd edn. Basingstoke: Palgrave Macmillan.

Rolfe, G., Freshwater, D. and Jasper, M. (2001) *Critical Reflection for Nursing and the Helping Professions: A user's guide.* Basingstoke: Palgrave Macmillan.

Ryum, T., Stiles, T.C., Svartberg, M. and McCullough, L. (2010) The role of transference work, the therapeutic alliance, and their interaction in reducing interpersonal problems among psychotherapy patients with Cluster C personality disorders, *Psychotherapy: Theory, Research, Practice, Training*, 47 (4): 442–53.

Sanders, P. (2006) *The Person-centred Counselling Primer.* Ross-on-Wye: PCCS Books.

Schön, D.A. (1983) *The Reflective Practitioner: How practitioners think in action.* New York: Basic Books.

Schön, D.A. (1987) *Educating the Reflective Practitioner: Toward a new design for teaching and learning in the professions.* San Francisco, CA: Jossey-Bass.

Smith, A. (1998) Learning about reflection, *Journal of Advanced Nursing*, 28 (4): 891–8.

Smith, E. (2011) Teaching critical reflection, *Teaching in Higher Education*, 16 (2): 211–23.

Tate, S. and Sills, M. (eds.) (2004) *The development of critical reflection in the health professions.* Occasional Paper #4. London: LTSN Centre for Health Sciences and Practice.

Taylor, B. (2000) *Reflective Practice: A guide for nurses and midwives.* Maidenhead: Open University Press.

Taylor, B. (2006) *Reflective Practice: A guide for nurses and midwives*, 2nd edn. Maidenhead: Open University Press.

Tee, S. and Newman, A. (2016) Principles of person-centred approaches to modern healthcare, in S. Tee (ed.) *Person-Centred Approaches in Healthcare: A handbook for nurses and midwives.* London: Open University Press.

Todd, G. (2002) The role of the internal supervisor in developing therapeutic nursing, in D. Freshwater (ed.) *Therapeutic Nursing:*

*Improving patient care through self-awareness and reflection.* London: Sage.

Todd, G. (2005) Reflective practice and Socratic dialogue, in T. Ghaye and S. Lillyman (eds.) *Effective Clinical Supervision: The role of reflection.* Dinton: Mark Allen Publishing.

Van Hooft, S., Gillam, L. and Byrnes, M. (1995) *Facts and Values: An introduction to critical thinking for nurses.* Sydney, NSW: MacLennan and Petty.

Van Manen, M. (1995) On the epistemology of reflective practice, *Teachers and Teaching: Theory and Practice*, 1 (1): 33–50.

Wells, A. (1997) Cognitive therapy for anxiety disorder, in C. Johns and D. Freshwater (eds.) *Transforming Nursing Through Reflective Practice*, 2nd edn. Oxford: Blackwell.

Wilkinson, J.M. (1996) *Nursing Process: A critical thinking approach.* Reading, MA: Addison-Wesley.

Wispé, L. (1986) The distinction between sympathy and empathy: a word is needed, *Journal of Personality and Social Psychology*, 50 (2): 314–21.

# Index

**Therapeutic Skills for Mental Health Nurses**

Evans and Hannigan

*ISBN: 9780335264407 (Paperback)*
*eISBN: 9780335264414*

*2016*

Most specialist mental health care is provided by nurses who use face-to-face helping skills with a wide range of people in a variety of contexts. This book puts therapeutic skills at the heart of the nurse's role, with one central aim: to equip you with knowledge to use in your practice, thus improving your ability to deliver care.

This book:

- Will enable you to strengthen your core therapeutic skills and broaden your knowledge to include other practical therapeutic approaches
- Collates in one place information on a range of therapeutic approaches, from person centred counselling, motivational interviewing and solution focused approaches, through to day-to-day skills of challenging unhelpful thoughts, de-escalating difficult situations, working with families, and problem solving
- Demonstrates application of theory to practice through a variety of practical examples
- Features reader activities to facilitate personal growth and learning
- Includes a chapter exploring clinical supervision and how this makes practice more effective

www.mheducation.co.uk

**COMPETENCIES FOR NURSING PRACTICE**
A Handbook for Student Nurses

Sheila Reading and Brian James Webster (Eds)

9780335246748 (Paperback)
August 2013

eBook also available

Achieving the NMC Competencies is an ongoing requirement that nurses work towards across all three years of pre-registration study. This book illuminates what students need to understand about each of the competencies and illustrates how best to achieve them in training and practice.

**Key features:**

- Each chapter tackles a different competency
- Uses activities and examples to help readers get to grips with the competency and relevant NMC requirements
- The book is very interactive and offers lot of portfolio activities for students to try, and use to demonstrate competency as they build a portfolio evidence

www.openup.co.uk